THE JOHNSON QU

THE JOHNSON QUOTATION BOOK

based on the collection of Chartres Biron

Edited with an introduction by

P.J. Smallwood

Bristol Classical Press

First published 1911 by Jonathan Cape.

This edition published in 1989 by
Bristol Classical Press
226 North Street
Bedminster
Bristol BS3 1JD

Introduction © P.J. Smallwood 1989

British Library Cataloguing in Publication Data

Johnson, Samuel, *1709-1784*
    ["Sir, said Dr Johnson"]. The Johnson
    quotation book; with an introduction by
    Philip Smallwood
    1. Quotations in English
    I. ["Sir, said Dr Johnson"] II. Title
    082

    ISBN 1-85399-065-5

Printed in Great Britain by
Billing & Sons Ltd, Worcester

Contents

Introduction	1
Children and Education	11
Marriage and the Affections	18
Work and the Professions	30
Friendship	45
Conversation	50
Eating and Drinking	60
Happiness	71
London	77
Scotland, Ireland and the Americans	81
Travel	86
The Whigs and Some Politicks	88
Political and other Economy	96
In General	102
Criticism Personal and Literary	116
Precept and Practice, and Religion	135
Death and his Own	142
Index	147

Introduction

Compared with the attention that they once received, Johnson's sayings are now often ignored, at least inside the academic world of 'Johnsonian Studies.' But outside 'Johnsonian Studies' (and outside the academic world) it is surely a different matter. For who does not know that "when a man is tired of London, he is tired of life"; that a second marriage is "the triumph of hope over experience"; that patriotism is "the last refuge of a scoundrel"? On the one hand, sayings of this kind are in a sense no longer Johnson's. They come from reported accounts of Johnson's talk. But they have something in common with examples of proverbial wisdom coined or preserved in literary form. They exist as 'literature'; but they have made the transition into the current of the language, and become part of it. Their 'truth' is familiar to those unaware of its source. On the other hand, the wide awareness of such sayings seems simultaneously to have helped to preserve the freshness of Johnson's popular, as distinct from his academic, appeal. The sayings of Johnson are part of a national stock. They are a public resource. They are the staple on which dictionaries of quotations, for example, still seem massively to rely. Johnson is grist to the mill for the authors of newspaper essays and broadcast talks. Their need for a controversial view, the necessity for some pithy comment to get discussion under way, make them remorseless, if predictable, quoters of Johnson's remarks. The result is that numerous people are acquainted with Johnson solely on account of his sayings. Within the academic world, it is as a writer, as a moralist and intellectual, and pre-eminently as a literary critic, that Johnson's reputation has recently flourished. The growth of this reputation has now eclipsed an older established 'academic' obsession with the biography of Johnson; with everything from Johnson's teapot to Johnson's cat. Outside its confines, where Johnson is remembered at all, he continues to be cherished for his rapid retorts, his witty aphorisms and ripostes 'on tap,' his instant opinions, darling prejudices and samples of wise humanity. Many and varied morsels of this kind are brought together, in categorized form, in the pages of this book. They range from thoughts on the education of the young to preparations for death; from how to combat personal grief to home truths about eating, drinking, and getting on with one's friends. Johnson's sayings have made him the greatest 'personality' in English literary history. This he remains. His one possible rival is Oscar Wilde.

Samuel Johnson was the son of a bookseller. He was born in 1709 at Lichfield in Staffordshire, but spent most of his life (like most successful literary men of his time) in London, where he talked and wrote until his death in 1784. Johnson's literary success has many different sides. He was an important poet (revered for many years after his death) and the author of two famous imitations of Juvenal's satires. He was a literary journalist, a key contributor to *The Gentleman's Magazine*, a reviewer, moral essayist, biographer, and in his early career, a Parliamentary reporter. He composed political pamphlets, including one of recently revived topical interest on the Falkland Islands. He edited Shakespeare. (Some of Johnson's notes to the plays are still preserved in the modern 'Arden' editions). And he compiled, single-handed, the first modern etymological dictionary of English. Johnson is one of the greatest of English literature's literary critics, an inspiration to Matthew Arnold and to T.S. Eliot. In this capacity he remains to this day a controversial figure. But Johnson's popular appeal, at least from the time of Macaulay, has always been that of the Man rather than that of the Writer. The two sides of Johnson's interest and importance have, of course, been frequently conflated. Johnson, even in his own time, was blamed as a Writer for his faults as a Man. For most people today, however, Johnson, while he may be respected for his literary productions, exists and is loved primarily as the larger-than-life figure from the pages of Boswell, his friend and biographer. An admiration for Johnson the Man, one derived from Boswell, lies behind this collection of the sayings. From a modern perspective, it seems in certain ways an exaggerated admiration, and symptomatic of an interest that has done Johnson no service at all. In other respects it is an important humanizing corrective in our conception of Johnson's intellectual achievement.

To call the entries in this volume 'sayings' is strictly inaccurate. Some are not sayings but anecdotes; they tell us about Johnson's life. Some are simply opinions, or reports of opinions. Some involve stretches of thinking longer than the term 'sayings' would tend to imply. Some consist of samples of dialogue, interesting as interactions rather than statements. Some are taken from Johnson's writings, even though, to quote Chartre Biron's original introduction to this collection, "The author obscures the man, the true Johnson is overlaid. It is in his talk that the artist in him finds expression." This comment reflects the 'period flavour' of Biron's collection. To preserve this flavour, and to capture a moment in the history of Johnson's reputation, the collection (minus its original introduction) is here reprinted intact. It was first published at a time when the appeal of Johnson the Man enjoyed a dominance that has now disappeared. A particular side of Johnson the Man comes to the surface. And it is one especially congenial to certain sections of turn-of-the-century taste. Aspects of this taste have always been part of Johnson's appeal. They still are. A high value, in some circles, is placed on the virtues of Johnsonian *bonhomie*. Johnson's 'clubbability' is still widely admired. These marks of an earlier taste form the basis of Biron's conception of Johnson.

They still attract many to Johnson, though they repel others. They are largely to do with a sense of Johnson the great Englishman-cum-eccentric, with the 'charm' of a plain-speaking crotchety temperamental 'character' who thought little of foreigners, held robust 'Tory' views, and was paradoxical though unshakeable in his powerful, oft-stated, convictions. Biron's collection of sayings plays up the endearing oddity, the singularity of Johnson. At times, in some sayings, Johnson seems very remote. He seems to be speaking from a completely alien set of social assumptions, attitudes and ideas. Some isolated remarks, doubtless, will at first view seem sexist and perhaps racist; though I believe that to think of them in this way is to misunderstand them. At other times, Biron seems to be selecting from Johnson so as to express prejudices of his own. This occurs when an attempt is made to give the sayings a kind of contemporary point by the sub-heading to which they are harnessed. Many of these sub-headings assist in universalizing Johnson's remarks. They turn them into morals of general proportions. But on occasion liberties are taken. Then, Biron appropriates Johnson as the mouthpiece for a *representative* selection of specifically Edwardian gentlemanly attitudes and values. Johnson is made to serve as the spokesman for a staunch independent Englishness and chauvinism that, if fashionable in 1911, is unfashionable now. "He may be right or wrong, dull or amusing, but it is England talking all the time." Except as a curiosity, or antiquity, (and some people have always regarded Johnson in this way) the Johnson who is "England talking" is nowadays likely to have a much more limited appeal.

The positive side of Biron's collection is its enthusiastic affection for Johnson the Man. This is the other current of the Boswellian legacy. It issues in the collection's relatively generous proportions. It is a collection which still offers one of the fullest available samples of Johnson's sayings assembled from more than one source. Here, mixed in with the remarks drawn unacknowledged from the writings of Johnson, we also find the Johnson whose conversation produced some of the English language's most quotable quotes. Johnson's *bons mots* were lovingly recorded, (and often sparked off), by his friends. Johnson, it is well known, made an art of 'talk'. Once securely established in his London literary career, he founded, for the purposes of conversation, the famous 'Literary Club'. The Club's membership comprised the most eminent figures of his day. *Habitués* of the circle include Gibbon, Burke, Reynolds, Warton, Goldsmith, Garrick, and of course Boswell. Each represents an important avenue of eighteenth-century intellectual, cultural and artistic life: history, politics, painting, literary criticism and scholarship, poetry, acting and bio-graphical writing – in that order. The sayings and pronouncements of Johnson extend to all these topics. The scope of this collection conveys something of the range and variety of Johnson's conversation. It suggests the diversity of Johnson's interests, inside and outside the world of letters. Whatever topic is in view, we catch a sense of the swiftness of his intellect at work, the alertness and creativeness of his wits. Johnson was often regarded, and to some extent still is, as a narrow or one-track mind, the oracle of stout but rather heavy Good Sense. But the sayings of Johnson reveal his mind's very unpredictable qualities; its agility, his tendency to move off in surprising directions; his delight in coming up with that which is not expected; his cultivation, for humorous reasons, of a system of *conscious* prejudices (such as the rude things he says about actors or the Scots), deliberately designed to needle his friends, to provoke them as only real friends can be provoked; his pleasure in 'talking for victory', the delight of mutually exclusive, contradictory points of view, so much the essence of life in the Club, but so frustrating for those engaged in fitting the Johnsonian philosophy of literature and life into the appropraite compartment of the History of Ideas.

The sayings reveal a consciously iconoclastic, subversive side to his nature that stands in marked contrast to the still popular (and for some, unattractive) image of Johnson the Anglican Tory. They reveal a lightness of heart, an ease and self-knowledge at odds with currently fashionable ideas of Johnson the post-Freudian fetishist and neurotic, the victim of impulses and appetites of which he was only just in control. In the face of ideas of this kind (a source of the principal academic interest that exists at the moment in Johnson the Man), it is salutary to find the sombre and austere moralist of *The Rambler* admitting that "If I had no duties, and no reference to futurity, I would spend my life in driving briskly in a post-chaise with a pretty woman." (p. 173). This does not mean, as it may be tempting to think, that the 'real' Johnson should be sought in the sayings, and that this Johnson is masked by the writings. The Johnson of the sayings complements the writer; he does not replace him. But qualities of writing (and reading) are apparent behind Johnson's 'conversational' self. And these add to its power to engage and alert. Much of the appeal of Johnson's short strokes, his conversational *coups*, is to be found in their epigrammatic compression, their 'turns'. There is often a certain reflexive quality in the sayings. The sentiment is made to turn back inwards on itself. It is something that recalls the high concentration of meaning to be found in certain lines from his poems:

> 'Sir, a man may be so much of every thing, that he is nothing of any thing.'

Moving from manner to matter, however, we see that Johnson's conversational remarks open access to opinions on topics not much discussed in his writings. In common with the writings, they introduce us to the various personalities of his day. But more than the writings, the sayings help capture the spirit and texture of day to day social relations, albeit of a very remarkable and singular kind. At the same time there is a sense in which they supplement the writings. Some key critical opinions are, for example, to be found in the conversational record: (Johnson's famous comparison of Fielding and Richardson is a notable case in point). Not all the conversational material is necessarily less serious, automatically more 'casual', than the published work. There are many passages, some included in this collection, where in speaking aloud Johnson has produced an extended train of reason and thought, a 'talk-paragraph' as it were. In such passages the mental 'grip' of Johnson is striking. The language is not quite that of speech. It is not 'public' in the sense of a Parliamentary oration. Nevertheless, in its control and direction, it provides a powerful contrast with modern, relatively sloppy, oratorical modes. It manifests a tenacity of mind which may remind us of the story of Johnson composing all the lines of his long poem, the *Vanity of Human Wishes*, before writing them down. The more obvious appeal of the sayings of Johnson is their acuteness, their vitality as charged examples of thinking on the spot. But the sayings are remarkable not just for their wit and quickness, their characteristic punch and 'delivery'. Such qualities are balanced by a moral grandeur and stability. As many entries in this edition reveal, there is a solidity and a coherence which links the talk to the writings. Seriousness of this kind must be among the merits that convinced Johnson's friends that Johnson's talk was worth recording in the first place; that it was something more than mere ephemeral conversation, and part of the whole substance of the man, not just a caricature or cartoon. It is true that at the other end of the scale, many of the remarks included in this collection seem to carry very little 'moral' point: there is one about 'The Advantages of Linen in a Seraglio'! The mingle of serious and trivial helps build the rounded character of Johnson. It invites us to construct, from the evidence of the conversation, a portrait of Johnson's mind, in formal and casual moods, that is satisfyingly complete, or would seem to be so. Johnson can reflect on the grandest of subjects, and on the most petty. He thus relates the profoundest matters of life to its daily concerns, its practical realities. This is a major triumph of Johnson's conversation. But it also fosters an illusion, one generated in the same way by this collection of sayings, by Boswell's *Life*, and by many biographical studies: i.e. that having the opinions of some person on many things creates the impression that there is no more to know. The talk is, however, merely one 'face' of Johnson. It is a fragment of the whole. The whole itself cannot be known; any more than, for that matter, it is possible entirely to 'know' anyone in real life.

This is not to say that Johnson did not consciously project a great deal of himself into his conversations. We know that he did. It was not a casual matter. One of his most famous 'sayings' is on conversation itself:

> No, Sir; we had *talk* enough, but no
> *conversation*; there was nothing *discussed*.

'Conversation' for Johnson, was a more structured event than is today usually conveyed by the term. It was also perhaps a less solemn, less stilted activity than what we would today call 'debate'. It was not *just* chat, but it had its affinities with play, in a form where rules and formalities are willingly obeyed, because they add to the pleasure, just as the rules of the heroic couplet both add to the sparkle and develop the profundity of Augustan verse. Many of the sayings seem deliberately to exaggerate the formality. Almost certainly, many of Johnson's best remarks are 'staged'. Boswell seems frequently to have regarded his role as 'straight man' to Johnson, goading his hero with provocations and prompts. To these he is primed ready to respond with his famous, half reproving, emphatic but half self-mocking prefatory 'Sir. . .'. There is evidence that, from time to time, Johnson wished Boswell would leave him alone. But he must surely have often cooperated in playing this game, and often enjoyed it. It is well known that Johnson's sayings were polished by Boswell, even if, when this had been done, the result was an even more convincingly personal and uniformly consistent 'Johnsonian' style. The famous Johnsonian manner is in part a tribute to Boswellian skill, as it is to the skill of those also responsible for recording Johnson's remarks: Mrs Thrale, Fanny Burney and others. The impression we receive of Johnson through their records of his talk is very much an effect of their art. They construct the personality whose sayings it is their ostensible object to preserve. Johnson himself, of course, provided the raw material. Only to a limited extent, then, is the character of Johnson a 'creation'.

We cannot, of course, know for sure what Johnson ever actually said. But here, in his sayings, recorded (and no doubt on many occasions adapted and embellished, if only in the spirit of their originator) lovingly and admiringly by his friends, we find the Samuel Johnson who it is often said (and rightly) seems so well to sum up the characteristically English wit, practical moral acuity, conversational vigour, and acid or affectionate humour of the eighteenth-century social and literary world. Perhaps for this very reason, the sayings of Johnson have presented an influential, albeit partial, and in the past excessively emphasised, view of his powers, one detrimental to an understanding and appreciation of his writings. We hear echoes in the sayings, but cannot (could not) actually find there the qualities of his major works: the creative fire and 'grip' of the *Vanity of Human Wishes*, the humanity and wisdom of *Rasselas*, the clarity, perception, intellectual energy, discrimination and emotional openness of his critical statements, especially in the *Preface to Shakespeare* (1765) and in the *Lives of the Poets* (1779-81). In his writings Johnson was much more than a man 'of his times'. But in his sayings, which in many ways take us back to a narrower eighteenth-century 'world', he has also achieved immortality. It is there we find the range of levels of interest, the diversity of preoccupations, that give human density and foundation to his literary and intellectual achievement, just as they give to his times the focussing reality and permanence of a body, a voice, and above all, a tone. So it is in the sayings that Johnson has continued to appeal freshly and directly to those whose interests are human rather than academic or literary. The wisdom of the sayings may be short-winded compared with that of the writings. But it is not peripheral to Johnson's achievement. It informs the writings and is informed by them. In their charm, humour, combativeness and provocation, the sayings contain much that the writings leave out. They are not the total picture (any more than the writings, and perhaps a good deal less). But they add substantially to it. More important than that is the human wisdom, in its own right, that they so humanly convey.

P.J. Smallwood, August 1988

Children and Education

One can scarcely help wishing while one fondles a baby that it may never live to become a man, for it is so probable that when he becomes a man he should end in a scoundrel. With girls, as their temptations are fewer, their virtues in this life and happiness in the next are less improbable, and I love to see a knot of little misses dearly.

THEIR REARING

'If, Sir, you were shut up in a castle, and a new-born child with you, what would you do?'

Johnson. 'Why, Sir, I should not much like my company.'

Boswell. 'But would you take the trouble of rearing it?' He seemed, as may be supposed, unwilling to pursue the subject; but upon my persevering in my question, replied, 'Why yes, Sir, I would; but I must have all conveniences. If I had no garden, I would make a shed on the roof, and take it there for fresh air. I should feed it, and wash it much, and with warm water to please it, not with cold water to give it pain.'

Boswell. 'But, Sir, does not heat relax?'

Johnson. 'Sir, you are not to imagine the water is to be very hot. I would not *coddle* the child. No, Sir, the hardy method of treating children does no good. I'll take you five children from London, who shall cuff five Highland children. Sir, a man bred in London will carry a burden, or run or wrestle, as well as a man brought up in the hardest manner in the country.'

11

TRUTH

Accustom your children constantly to this; if a thing happened at one window and they when relating it say it happened at another, do not let it pass but instantly check them. You do not know where deviation from Truth will end.

THEIR READING

Babies do not want to hear about babies, they like to be told of giants and castles and of somewhat which can stretch and stimulate their little minds.

ITS CHOICE

'I would put a child into a library (where no unfit books are) and let him read at his choice. A child should not be discouraged from reading anything he takes a liking to, from a notion that it is above his reach. If that be the case, the child will soon find it out and desist; if not he of course gains the instruction; which is so much the more likely to come, from the inclination with which he takes up the study.'

ARITHMETIC

Let your boy learn arithmetic, he will not then be a prey to every rascal which this town swarms with. Teach him the value of money and how to reckon it. Ignorance to a wealthy lad of one and twenty is only so much fat to a sick sheep, it just serves to call the rooks about him.

PUBLIC SCHOOLS

'More is learned in public than in private schools, from emulation: there is the collision of mind with mind, or the radiation of many minds pointing to one centre. Though few boys make their own exercises, yet if a good exercise is given up, out of a great number of boys, it is made by somebody.'

'I hate by-roads in education. Education is as well known, and has long been as well known, as ever it can be. Endeavouring to make children prematurely wise is useless labour.

Suppose they have more knowledge at five or six years old than other children, what use can be made of it? It will be lost before it is wanted, and the waste of so much time and labour of the teacher can never be repaid. Too much is expected from precocity, and too little performed. Miss ——— was an instance of early cultivation, but in what did it terminate? In marrying a little Presbyterian parson, who keeps an infant boarding-school, so that all her employment now is, "To suckle fools, and chronicle small beer." She tells the children, "This is a cat, and that is a dog, with four legs and a tail; see there! you are much better than a cat or a dog, for you can speak." If I had bestowed such an education on a daughter, and had discovered that she thought of marrying such a fellow, I would have sent her to the *Congress*.'

FOR A TIMID BOY

Sir, this is a preposterous expedient for removing his infirmity. Such a disposition should be cultivated in the shade. Placing him at a public school is forcing an owl upon day.

OVER-REFINEMENT IN EDUCATION

Johnson advised me to-night not to *refine* in the education of my children. 'Life will not bear refinement; you must do as other people do.'

LECTURES

'People have nowadays got a strange opinion that every thing should be taught by lectures. Now, I cannot see that lectures can do so much good as reading the books from which the lectures are taken. I know nothing that can be best taught by lectures, except where experiments are to be shown. You may teach chemistry by lectures. – You might teach making of shoes by lectures!'

PUNISHMENT

'I would rather have the rod to be the general terror to all, to make them learn, than tell a child, if you do thus, or thus, you will be more esteemed than your brothers or sisters. The rod produces an effect which terminates in itself. A child is afraid of being whipped, and gets his task, and there's an end on't; whereas, by exciting emulation and comparisons of superiority, you lay the foundation of lasting mischief; you make brothers and sisters hate each other.'

When Johnson saw some young ladies in Lincolnshire who were remarkably well behaved, owing to their mother's strict discipline and severe correction, he exclaimed, in one of Shakespeare's lines, a little varied:

'Rod, I will honour thee for this thy duty.'

LOSS AND GAIN

There is now less flogging in our great schools than formerly, but then less is learned there; so that what the boys get at one end they lose at the other.

CHILDREN

'There is no matter what you teach them first – it matters no more than which leg you put first into your breeches – Sir, you may stand disputing which you shall put in first, but in the meantime your legs are bare – No matter which you put in first so that you put them both in, and then you have your breeches on. Sir, while you think which of two things to teach a child first, another boy in the common course has learned both.'

A TASTE FOR READING

'I am always for getting a boy forward in his learning; for that is a sure good. I would let him at first read *any* English book which happens to engage his attention; because you have done a great deal, when you have brought him to have entertainment from a book. He'll get better books afterwards.'

DESULTORY READING

'It has been by that means that all my knowledge has been

gained, except what I have picked up by running about the world with my wits ready to observe and my tongue ready to talk. A man is seldom in a humour to unlock his bookcase, set his desk in order, and betake himself to serious study, but a retentive memory will do something and a fellow shall have strange credit given him if he can but recollect striking passages from different books, keep the author separate in his head, and bring his stock of knowledge artfully into play; how else do the gamesters manage when they play for more money than they are worth?'

INCLINATION
For general improvement a man should read whatever his immediate inclination prompts him to. What we read with inclination makes a much stronger impression. If we read without inclination, half the mind is employed in fixing the attention, so there is but one half to be employed on what we read.

THE FOUNDATION OF LEARNING
The foundation of learning must be laid by reading. General principles must be had from books which, however, must be brought to the test of real life. In conversation you never get a system. What is said upon a subject is to be gathered from a hundred people. The parts of a truth which a man gets thus, are at such a distance from each other that he never attains to a full view.

READERS RARE
It is strange there should be so little reading in the world and so much writing. People in general do not read if they can have anything else to amuse them. There must be an external impulse – emulation or vanity or avarice. The progress which the understanding makes through a book has more pain than pleasure in it. Language is scanty and inadequate to express the nice gradations and mixtures of our feelings. No man reads a book of science from pure inclination. The books that we do read with pleasure are light compositions which contain a quick

succession of events.

YOUTHFUL IMPRESSIONS

Little people should be encouraged always to tell whatever they hear particularly striking to some brother, sister or servant, immediately before the impression is erased by the intervention of newer occurrences. I perfectly remember the first time I ever heard of Heaven and Hell, because when my mother had made out such a description of both places as she thought likely to seize the attention of her infant auditor who was then in bed with her, she got up and, dressing me before the usual time, sent me directly to call a favourite workman in the house to whom she knew I would communicate the conversation while it was yet impressed on my mind. The event was what she wished, and it was to that method I think I chiefly owe my uncommon felicity in distant occurrences and long-past conversations.

THE USE OF BOARDING SCHOOLS

Boarding schools were established for the conjugal quiet of the parents. The two partners cannot agree which child to fondle nor how to fondle them, so they put the young ones to school and remove the cause of contention. The little girl pokes her head, the mother reproves her sharply: 'Do not mind your mamma,' says the father, 'my dear, but do your own way.' The mother complains to me of this. 'Madam,' said I, 'your husband is right all the while, he is with you but two hours of the day perhaps and then you tease him by making the child cry. Are not ten hours enough for tuition, and are the hours of pleasure so frequent in life that when a man gets a couple of quiet ones to spend in familiar chat with his wife they must be poisoned by petty mortification. Put missey to school; she will have to hold her head like her neighbours and you will no longer torment your family for want of other talk.'

THE CHILDREN OF SCHOOLMASTERS

That lad looks like the son of a schoolmaster, which is one of the very worst conditions of childhood. Such a boy has no father or worse than none, he never can reflect on his parent but the reflection brings to his mind some idea of pain inflicted or of sorrow suffered.

IF HE HAD HAD CHILDREN

I hope I should have willingly lived on bread and water to obtain instruction for these, but I would not have set their future friendship to hazard for the sake of thrusting into their heads knowledge of things for which they might not perhaps have either taste or necessity. You teach your daughters the diameters of the planets, and wonder when you have done that they do not delight in your company. No science can be communicated by mortal creatures without attention from the scholar. No attention can be obtained from children without the infliction of pain, and pain is never remembered without resentment.

ON THE RESPECTIVE MERITS OF TWO INFANT RECITERS

'No pray, Sir, let the little dears both speak it at once. More noise will by that means be made and the noise will be the sooner over.'

Marriage and the Affections

HIS OWN
'Sir, it was a love marriage on both sides.'

ON THE WAY TO THE WEDDING
'Sir, she had read the old romances, and had got into her
head the fantastical notion that a woman of spirit should use her
lover like a dog. So, Sir, at first she told me that I rode too fast,
and she could not keep up with me; and, when I rode a little
slower, she passed me, and complained that I lagged behind. I
was not to be made the slave of caprice; and I resolved to begin
as I meant to end. I therefore pushed on briskly, till I was fairly
out of her sight. The road lay between two hedges, so I was sure
she could not miss it; and I contrived that she should soon come
up with me. When she did, I observed her to be in tears.'

IN ANSWER TO MRS. THRALE
I asked Mr. Johnson if he ever disputed with his wife.
'Perpetually,' said he. 'My wife had a particular reverence for
cleanliness and deserved the praise of neatness in her dress and
furniture as many ladies do till they become troublesome to their
best friends, slaves to their own besoms and only sigh for the
hour of sweeping their husbands out of the house as dirt and
useless lumber. "A clean floor is so comfortable," she would say
sometimes by way of twitting, till at last I told her that I thought
we had talk enough about the floor, we would now have a touch
at the ceiling.' I asked him if he ever huffed his wife about his
dinner.

'So often,' replied he, 'that at last she called to me and said, "Nay hold, Mr. Johnson, and do not make a farce of thanking God for a dinner which in a few minutes you will protest not eatable." '

HIS FIRST LOVE

'You will see, Sir, at Mr. Hector's, his sister, Mrs. Careless, a clergyman's widow. She was the first woman with whom I was in love. It dropt out of my head imperceptibly; but she and I shall always have a kindness for each other.'

THE CHOICE

When he again talked of Mrs. Careless tonight, he seemed to have had his affection revived;, for he said, 'If I had married her, it might have been as happy for me.'

Boswell. 'Pray, Sir, do you not suppose that there are fifty women in the world, with any one of whom a man may be as happy, as with any one woman in particular?'

Johnson. 'Aye, Sir, fifty thousand.'

Boswell. 'Then, Sir, you are not of opinion with some who imagine that certain men and certain women are made for each other; and that they cannot be happy if they miss their counterparts.'

Johnson. 'To be sure not, Sir. I believe marriages would in general be as happy, and often more so, if they were all made by the Lord Chancellor, upon a due consideration of the characters and circumstances, without the parties having any choice in the matter.'

THE HAPPIEST PERIOD OF HIS LIFE

It was that year in which I spent one whole evening with Molly Aston. That indeed was not happiness, it was rapture, but thoughts of it sweetened the whole year. Molly was a beauty and a scholar and a wit and a Whig and she talked all in praise of liberty, and so I made this epigram upon her. She was the loveliest creature I ever saw, 'Liber ut esse velim, suasisti pulera Maria ut maneam liber, pulera Maria, vale.' 'How will it do this way in English?' said I (Mrs. Thrale). 'Persuasions to freedom fall oddly from you. If freedom we seek, fair Maria, adieu.' It will do well enough but it is translated by a lady, and the ladies never loved Molly Aston.

WHAT MRS. JOHNSON THOUGHT OF IT

She was jealous to be sure and teased me sometimes when I would let her, and one day, as a fortune-telling gipsy passed us, when we were walking out in company with two or three friends in the country, she made the wench look at my hand, but soon repented her curiosity, for, says the gipsy, your heart is divided, Sir, between a Betty and a Molly. Betty loves you best but you take most delight in Molly's company. When I turned about to laugh I saw my wife was crying. Pretty charmer she had no reason.

LOVE

A passion which he who never felt never was happy, and he who laughs at never deserves to feel. A passion which has caused the change of empires and the loss of worlds, a passion which has inspired heroism and subdued avarice.

A DEFINITION

'Love is the wisdom of the fool and the folly of the wise.'

ITS EFFECTS

Of the passion of love he remarked, that its violence and ill effects were much exaggerated; for who knows any real sufferings on that head, more than from the exorbitancy of any other passion?

FALLING IN LOVE

If you could shut up any man with any woman so as to make them derive their whole pleasure from each other, they would inevitably fall in love as it is called with each other, but at six months' end if you would throw them both into public life where they might change partners at leisure, each would soon forget that fondness which mutual dependence and the paucity of general amusement alone had caused, and each would feel separately delighted by their release.

A DISTINCTION

'But love and marriage are different states. Those who are to suffer the evils together, and to suffer often for the sake of one another, soon lose that tenderness of look, and that ben-evolence of mind, which arose from the participation of unmingled pleasure and successive amusement. A woman, we are sure, will not be always fair; we are not sure she will always be virtuous: and a man cannot retain through life that respect and assiduity by which he pleases for a day or for a month. I do not, however, pretend to have discovered that life has any thing more to be desired than a prudent and virtuous marriage; therefore I know not what counsel to give you.'

ITS RITUAL

'Our marriage service is too refined. It is calculated only for the best kind of marriages; whereas, we should have a form for matches of convenience, of which there are many.'

UNDUE EXPECTATION

'Now that you are going to marry, do not expect more from life than life will afford. You may often find yourself out of humour, and you may often think your wife not studious enough to please you; and yet you may have reason to consider yourself as upon the whole very happily married.'

BEAUTY

'Sir, it is a very foolish resolution to resolve not to marry a pretty woman. Beauty is of itself very estimable. No, Sir, I would prefer a pretty woman, unless there are objections to her. A pretty woman may be foolish; a pretty woman may be wicked; a pretty woman may not like me. But there is no such danger in marrying a pretty woman as is apprehended; she will not be persecuted if she does not invite persecution. A pretty woman, if she has a mind to be wicked, can find a readier way than another; and that is all.'

THE GOOD WE KNOW
Do not forbear to marry a beautiful woman if you can find such, out of a fancy that she will be less constant than an ugly one, or condemn yourself to the society of coarseness and vulgarity for fear of the expenses or other dangers of elegance and personal charms, which have always been acknowledged a positive good, and for the want of which there should always be given some weighty compensation.

I have however seen some prudent fellows who forbore to connect themselves with beauty lest coquetry should be near, and with art or birth lest insolence should lurk behind them, till they have been forced by their discretion to linger life away in tasteless stupidity and choose to count the moments by remembrance of pain instead of enjoyment of pleasure.

FOR MEN
'Marriage is the best state for man in general; and every man is a worse man, in proportion as he is unfit for the married state.'

REASONS FOR MATRIMONY
A man should marry first for virtue, secondly for wit, thirdly for beauty, and fourthly for money.

RELIGIOUS WIVES
A principle of honour or fear of the world will many times keep a man in decent order, but when a woman loses her religion she in general loses the only tie that will restrain her actions.

FOR WOMEN

'Marriage, Sir, is much more necessary to a man than to a woman: for he is much less able to supply himself with domestic comforts. You will recollect my saying to some ladies the other day, that I had often wondered why young women should marry, as they have so much more freedom, and so much more attention paid to them, while unmarried, than when married. I indeed did not mention the *strong* reason for their marrying – the *mechanical* reason.'

Boswell. 'Why that is a strong one, but does not imagination make it much more important than it is in reality? Is it not to a certain degree a delusion in us as well as in women?'

Johnson. 'Why yes, Sir, but it is a delusion which is always beginning again.'

Boswell. 'I do not know but there is on the whole more misery than happiness produced by that passion.'

Johnson. 'I do not think so, Sir.'

MARRYING FOR LOVE

'It is commonly a weak man who marries for love.' We then talked of marrying women of fortune; and I mentioned a common remark, that a man may be, upon the whole, richer by marrying a woman with a very small portion, because a woman of fortune will be proportionately expensive; whereas a woman who brings none will be very moderate in expenses.

Johnson. 'Depend upon it, Sir, this is not true. A woman of fortune being used to the handling of money, spends it judiciously: but a woman who gets the command of money for the first time upon her marriage, has such a gust in spending it that she throws it away with great profusion.'

WIVES AND BUSINESS

It was well managed of him to leave his affairs in the hands of his wife, because in matters of business no woman stops at integrity.

DRESS ALLOWANCE
'Yes, Sir; no money is better spent than what is laid out for domestic satisfaction. A man is pleased that his wife is drest as well as other people; and a wife is pleased that she is drest.'

ON CHOOSING PRESENTS
If a wench wants a good gown do not give her a fine smelling-bottle because that is more delicate, as I once knew a lady lend the key of her library to a poor scribbling dependent as if she took the woman for an ostrich that could digest iron.

MARRYING BENEATH YOU
'Were I a man of rank I would not let a daughter starve who had made a mean marriage; but having voluntarily degraded herself from the station which she was originally entitled to hold, I would support her only in that which she herself had chosen; and would not put her on a level with my other daughters. You are to consider, Madam, that it is our duty to maintain the subordination of civilised society; and when there is a gross and shameful deviation from rank, it should be punished so as to deter others from the same perversion.'

MARRYING A FOOL
A man of sense and education should meet a suitable companion in a wife. It was a miserable thing when the conversation could only be such as, whether the mutton should be boiled or roasted, and probably a dispute about that.

MENTAL AND OTHER FOOD
A man is in general better pleased when he has a good dinner on his table than when his wife talks Greek.

MARRYING A STUDENT
'Supposing a wife to be of a studious or argumentative turn, it would be very troublesome: for instance, if a woman should

continually dwell upon the Arian heresy.'*

ADVICE TO AN IMPORTUNATE YOUNG GENTLEMAN
'Mr. Johnson, would you advise me to marry?'

'Sir, I would advise no man to marry who is not likely to propagate understanding.'

ON MARRYING AGAIN
'By taking a second wife he pays the highest compliment to the first, by showing that she made him so happy as a married man, that he wishes to be so a second time.'

A SECOND MARRIAGE
It is the triumph of hope over experience.

MATRIMONIAL QUARRELS
All quarrels ought to be avoided studiously, particularly conjugal ones, as no one can possibly tell where they may end; besides that, lasting dislike is often the consequence of occasional disgust, and the cup of life is surely bitter enough without squeezing in the hateful rind of resentment.

ON BEING SUPPLANTED
'I do not see, Sir, that it is reasonable for a man to be angry at another, whom a woman has preferred to him: but angry he is, no doubt: and he is loth to be angry at himself.'

LATE MARRIAGES
He did not approve of late marriages, observing that more was lost in point of time than compensated for by any possible advantages. Even ill-assorted marriages were preferable to cheerless celibacy.

THEIR OFFSPRING
The unhappy produce of them becomes the plaything of

* the Arian heresy: A famous heresy, originating from Arius in the 4th Century who denied that God and Jesus Christ were consubstantial.

dotage: an old man's child leads much such a life I think as a little boy's dog, teased with awkward fondness and forced to sit up and beg, as we call it, to divert a company, who at last go away complaining of their disagreeable entertainment.

AN UNNATURAL STATE

'Sir, it is so far from being natural for a man and woman to live in a state of marriage, that we find all the motives which they have for remaining in that connection, and the restraints which civilised society imposes to prevent separation, are hardly sufficient to keep them together.'

THE SEVENTH COMMANDMENT

'Confusion of progeny constitutes the essence of the crime; and therefore a woman who breaks her marriage vows is much more criminal than a man who does it. A man, to be sure, is criminal in the sight of God; but he does not do his wife a material injury, if he does not insult her; if, for instance, from mere wantonness of appetite, he steals privately to her chamber-maid. Sir, a wife ought not greatly to resent this. I would not receive home a daughter who had run away from her husband on that account. A wife should study to reclaim her husband by more attention to please him. Sir, a man will not, once in a hundred instances, leave his wife and go to a harlot, if his wife has not been negligent of pleasing.'

COMPLAISANCE

'This is miserable stuff, Sir. To the contract of marriage, besides the man and wife, there is a third party – Society; and if it be considered as a vow – GOD: and, therefore, it cannot be dissolved by their consent alone. Laws are not made for particular cases, but for men in general. A woman may be unhappy with her husband; but she cannot be freed from him without the approbation of the civil and ecclesiastical power. A man may be unhappy, because he is not so rich as another; but he is not to seize upon another's property with his own hand.'

Boswell. 'But, Sir, this lady does not want that the contract should be dissolved; she only argues that she may indulge herself in gallantries with equal freedom as her husband does provided she takes care not to introduce a spurious issue into his family. You know, Sir, what Macrobius has told of Julia.'

Johnson. 'This lady of yours, Sir, I think, is very fit for a brothel.'

ON A LADY WITH TEMPERAMENT
'My dear Sir, never accustom your mind to mingle virtue and vice. The woman's a whore, and there's an end on't.'

HUSBANDS AND WIVES
'Between a man and his Maker it is a different question: but between a man and a wife, a husband's infidelity is nothing. They are connected by children, by fortune, by serious considerations of community. Wise married women don't trouble themselves about infidelity in their husbands.'

'The difference is boundless. The man imposes no bastards upon his wife.'

THEIR TEMPTATION
'Women have not the same temptations that we have; they may always live in virtuous company. Men must mix in the world indiscriminately.'

A MISTAKE
'Some cunning men choose fools for their wives, thinking to manage them, but they always fail. There is a spaniel fool and a mule fool. The spaniel fool may be made to do by beating. The mule fool will neither do by words or blows; and the spaniel fool often turns mule at last; and suppose a fool to be made do pretty well, you must have the continual trouble of making her do. Depend upon it, no woman is the worse for sense and knowledge.'

MAN AND SUPERMAN

'Men know that women are an over-match for them, and therefore they choose the weakest or most ignorant. If they did not think so, they never could be afraid of women knowing as much as themselves.'

FORTUNE-HUNTERS

He observed, a principal source of erroneous judgment was, viewing things partially and only on *one side*: as, for instance, *fortune-hunters*, when they contemplated the fortunes *singly* and *separately* it was a dazzling and tempting object; but when they came to possess the wives and their fortunes *together*, they began to suspect they had not made quite so good a bargain.

MARRYING MONEY

Now has that fellow at length obtained the certainty of three meals a day, and for that certainty, like the brother dog in the fable, he will get his neck galled for life with a collar.

IN OUR HOURS OF EASE

Women give great offence by a contemptuous spirit of non-compliance on petty occasions. The man calls his wife to walk with him in the shade, and she feels a strange desire just at that moment to sit in the sun. He offers to read her a play or sing her a song and she calls the children in to disturb them, or addresses him to seize that opportunity of settling the family accounts.

Twenty such tricks will the faithfullest wife in the world not refuse to play and then look astonished when the fellow fetches in a mistress.

QUALITY

'High people, Sir, are the best; take a hundred ladies of quality, you'll find them better wives, better mothers, more willing to sacrifice their own pleasure to their children, than a hundred other women. Tradeswomen (I mean the wives of tradesmen) in the city, who are worth from £10,000 to £15,000, are the worst creatures upon the earth, grossly ignorant, and thinking viciousness fashionable. Farmers, I think, are often worthless fellows. Few lords will cheat; and, if they do, they'll be ashamed of it; farmers cheat and are not ashamed of it: they have all the sensual vices too of the nobility, with cheating into the bargain. There is as much fornication and adultery amongst farmers as amongst noblemen.'

Boswell. 'The notion of the world, Sir, however, is that the morals of women of quality are worse than those in lower stations.'

Johnson. 'Yes, Sir, the licentiousness of one woman of quality makes more noise than that of a number of women in lower stations; then, Sir, you are to consider the malignity of women in the city against women of quality, which will make them believe anything of them, such as that they call their coachmen to bed. No, Sir, so far as I have observed, the higher in rank the richer ladies are, they are the better instructed and the more virtuous.'

IMAGINATION

'Were it not for imagination, Sir, a man would be as happy in the arms of a Chambermaid as of a Duchess. But such is the adventitious charm of fancy, that we find men who have violated the best principles of society, and ruined their fame and their fortune, that they might possess a woman of rank.'

A COUNTESS

'Sir, if I had an amour it should be with a countess; it would fire the imagination.'

THE ADVANTAGES OF LINEN IN A SERAGLIO

'I have often thought, that, if I kept a seraglio, the ladies should all wear linen gowns, – or cotton; – I mean stuffs made of vegetable substances. I would have no silk; you cannot tell when it is clean: It will be very nasty before it is perceived to be so. Linen detects its own dirtiness.'

Work and the Professions

THE MISFORTUNE
The greatest misfortune that can befall a man is to have been bred to no profession.

WORK
'Employment, Sir, and hardships prevent melancholy. I suppose in all our army in America there was not one man who went mad.'

IDLENESS
'Sir, you cannot give me an instance of any man who is permitted to lay out his own time, contriving not to have tedious hours.'

THE RECURRENT TALLOW-CHANDLER
'An eminent tallow-chandler in London, who had acquired a considerable fortune, gave the trade in favour of his foreman, and went to live at a country-house near town. He soon grew weary, and paid frequent visits to his old shop, where he desired they might let him know their *melting-days*, and he would come and assist them; which he accordingly did. Here, Sir, was a man, to whom the most disgusting* circumstance in the business to which he had been used, was a relief from idleness.'

MUSIC
'If he had learnt music, he should have been afraid he

---

* disgusting: i.e. in the eighteenth-century sense, meaning distasteful.

would have done nothing else but play. It was a method of employing the mind, without the labour of thinking at all, and with some applause from a man's self.'

ON PLAYING THE VIOLIN
Difficult do you call it, Sir? I wish it were impossible.

ITS MORAL ASPECT
'Music is the only sensual pleasure without vice.'

ITS EFFECT
'This is the first time that I have ever been affected by musical sounds, the impression made upon me is of a melancholy kind.'

ITS SUGGESTION
It excites in my mind no ideas and hinders me from contemplating my own.

MONEY MAKING
'There are few ways in which a man can be more innocently employed than in getting money.'

CHOOSING A PROFESSION
That so many objections might be made to everything, that nothing could overcome them but the necessity of doing something. No man would be of any profession, as simply opposed to not being of it: but everyone must do something.

THE IDEAL BUSINESS
Scorn to put your behaviour under the dominion of canters. Never think it clever to call physic a mean study, or law a dry one, or ask a babe of seven years old which way his genius leads him, when we all know a boy of seven years has no genius for anything except a peg-top and and apple pye, but fix upon some business where much money may be got and little virtue risked.

ADVICE TO MR. WINDHAM ON BECOMING SECRETARY TO THE
LORD LIEUTENANT OF IRELAND

I have no timidity in my own disposition and am no
encourager of it in others. Never be afraid to think yourself fit
for anything for which your friends think you fit. You will
become an able negotiator – a very pretty rascal. No one in
Ireland wears even the mark of incorruption. No one professes
to do for sixpence what he can get a shilling for doing. Set sail
and see where the winds and waves will carry you.

THE ETHICS OF ADVOCACY

'Sir, a lawyer has no business with the justice or injustice
of the cause which he undertakes, unless his client asks his
opinion, and then he is bound to give it honestly. The justice or
injustice of the cause is to be decided by the judge. Consider,
Sir; what is the purpose of courts of justice? It is, that every man
may have his cause fairly tried, by men appointed to try causes.
A lawyer is not to tell what he knows to be a lie: he is not to
produce what he knows to be a false deed; but he is not to usurp
the province of the jury and of the judge and determine what
shall be the effect of evidence, – what shall be the result of legal
argument. As it rarely happens that a man is fit to plead his own
cause, lawyers are a class of the community, who, by study and
experience, have acquired the art and power of arranging
evidence, and of applying to the points at issue what the law has
settled. A lawyer is to do for his client all that his client might
fairly do for himself, if he could. If, by a superiority of attention,
of knowledge, of skill, and a better method of communication,
he has the advantage of his adversary, it is an advantage to which
he is entitled. There must always be some advantage, on one side
or other; and it is better that advantage should be had by talents
than by chance. If lawyers were to undertake no causes till they
were sure they were just, a man might be precluded altogether
from a trial of his claim, though, were it judicially examined, it
might be found a very just claim.'

ADVOCACY AND RIGHT FEELING

Boswell. 'I asked him whether as a moralist he did not think that the practice of the law in some respect hurt the true feeling of honesty.'

Johnson. 'Why no, Sir! if you act properly. You are not to deceive your clients with false representation of your opinion, you are not to tell lies to a judge.'

Boswell. ' But what do you think of supporting a cause which you know to be bad?'

Johnson. 'Sir, you do not know it to be good or bad till the judge determines it. I have said you are to state facts fairly, so that your thinking, or what you call knowing, a cause to be bad must be from reasoning, must be from supposing your arguments to be weak and inconclusive. But, Sir, that is not enough. An argument which does not convince yourself may convince the judge to whom you urge it, and if it does convince him why then, Sir, you are wrong, and he is right. It is his business to judge, and you are not to be confident in your opinion that a cause is bad, but to say all you can for your client and then hear the judge's opinion.'

Boswell. 'But, Sir, does not affecting a warmth when you have no warmth, and appearing to be clearly of the opinion when you are in reality of another opinion, does not such dissimulation impair one's honesty? Is there not some danger that a lawyer may put on the same mark in common life in the intercourse with his friends.'

Johnson. 'Why no, Sir. Everybody knows you are paid for affecting warmth for your client and it is therefore properly no dissimulation. The moment you come from the bar you resume your usual behaviour. Sir, a man will no more bring the artifice of the bar into the common intercourse of society than a man who is paid for tumbling upon his hands will continue to tumble on his hands when he should walk on his feet.'

ITS PROSPECTS

'You must not indulge too sanguine hopes, should you be called to our bar. I was told, by a very sensible lawyer, that there are a great many chances against any man's success in the profession of the law: the candidates are so numerous, and those who get large practice so few. He said it was by no means true that a man of good parts and application is sure of having business, though he indeed allowed that if such a man could but appear in a few causes, his merit would be known, and he would get forward; but that the great risk was, that a man might pass half a life-time in the Courts, and never have an opportunity of showing his abilities.'

JUDGES AND THEIR AVOCATIONS

Sir, you may as well say a judge should not have a house, for they may come and tell him, 'Your Lordship's house is on fire,' and so instead of minding the business of his Court, he is to be occupied in getting the engine with the greatest speed. There is no end of this. Every judge who has land trades to a certain extent in corn or in cattle and in the land itself undoubtedly. His steward acts for him, and so do clerks for a great merchant. A judge may be a farmer but he is not to geld his own pigs. A judge may play a little at cards for his amusement, but he is not to play at marbles or chuck farthing in the piazza. No, Sir, there is no profession to which a man gives a very great proportion of his time. It is wonderful when a calculation is made how little the mind is actually employed in the discharge of any profession. No man would be a judge upon the condition of being totally a judge. The best employed lawyer has his mind at work but for a small proportion of his time.

THE LAW

The Law is the last result of human wisdom acting upon human experience for the benefit of the public.

ANTIQUARIES
A mere antiquarian is a rugged being.

ATTORNEYS
I would be loth to speak ill of any person, who I do not know deserves it, but I am afraid he is an attorney.

WRITING
'No man but a blockhead ever wrote, except for money.'

INSPIRATION IN LITERATURE
'What *must* be done, Sir, *will* be done.'

DOGGED DOES IT
'A man may write at any time, if he will set himself doggedly to it.'

EASY WRITING
What is written without effort is in general read without pleasure.

A CERTAIN FEMALE WRITER
'She is better employed at her toilet, than using her pen. It is better she should be reddening her own cheeks, than blackening other people's characters.'

CERTAIN FEMALE WRITERS*
'Literature is not often worse employed than in dignifying the amorous folly of a raving girl.'

SEX APPEAL
'Love has no great influence on the sum of Life.'

---

* Certain Female Writers: Johnson was not attacking 'female writers'. The remark comes from his 'Life of Pope' (1781) and refers to the suicidal heroine of Pope's poem 'An Elegy to the Memory of an Unfortunate Lady'. Johnson has 'fury' not 'folly'.

TO A LADY WHO HAD WRITTEN A TRAGEDY BUT 'HAD SO
MANY IRONS IN THE FIRE'
Why then, Madam, the best thing I can advise you to do is
put your tragedy along with your irons.

HISTORIANS
'Great abilities are not requisite for an Historian; for, in
historical composition, all the greatest powers of the human
mind are quiescent. He has facts ready to his hand; so there is
no exercise of invention. Imagination is not required in any high
degree; only about as much as is used in the lower kinds of
poetry. Some penetration, accuracy, and colouring, will fit a
man for the task, if he can give the application which is
necessary.'

CRITICS
'I would rather be attacked than unnoticed. For the worst
thing you can do to an author is to be silent as to his works. An
assault upon a town is a bad thing; but starving it is still worse;
an assault may be unsuccessful; you may have more men killed
than you kill; but if you starve the town, you are sure of victory.'

ITS EFFECT
Attacks on authors did them much service. 'A man who
tells me my play is very bad, is less my enemy than he who lets it
die in silence. A man, whose business it is to be talked of, is much
helped by being attacked.'

FAME
'It is advantageous to an author, that his book should be
attacked as well as praised. Fame is a shuttlecock. If it be struck
only at one end of the room, it will soon fall to the ground. To
keep it up, it must be struck at both ends.'

THE REAL CRITIC
A man who writes a book thinks himself wiser or wittier
than the rest of mankind, he supposes he can instruct and amuse

them, and the public to whom he appeals must, after all, be the judges of his pretensions.

THE BEST JUDGES

There are three distinct kinds of judges on all new authors or productions. The first are those who know no rules but pronounce entirely from their natural taste and feelings. The second are those who know and judge by rules. The third are those who know but are above the rules. The last are those you should wish to satisfy. Next to them rate the natural judges, but ever despise those opinions that are formed by the rules. The natural feelings of untaught hearers ought never to be slighted.

ON BEING INTRODUCED TO AUTHORS

'Dearest Madam, you had better let it alone. The best part of every author is in general to be found in his book.'

ON CANDOUR TO AUTHORS

'Very true, Sir. Therefore the man who is asked by an author what he thinks of his work, is put to the torture, and is not obliged to speak the truth; so that what he says is not considered as his opinion.'

CANDOUR AMONGST AUTHORS

'The reciprocal civility of authors is one of the most risible scenes in the farce of Life.'

THE ARMY

'It is wonderful how ignorant many officers of the army are considering how much leisure they have for study and the acquisition of knowledge.'

ITS MANNERS

Perfect good breeding 'consists in having no particular mark of any profession, but a general elegance of manners; whereas, in a military man, you can commonly distinguish the *brand* of a soldier, *l'homme d'épée.*'

ITS ATTRACTION

We talked of war. *Johnson*. 'Every man thinks meanly of himself for not having been a soldier, or not having been at sea.' *Boswell*. 'Lord Mansfield does not.' *Johnson*. 'Sir, if Lord Mansfield were in a company of General Officers and Admirals who have been in service, he would shrink; he'd wish to creep under the table.' *Boswell*. 'No; he'd think he could *try* them all.' *Johnson*. 'Yes, if he could catch them: but they'd try him much sooner. No, Sir; were Socrates and Charles the Twelfth of Sweden both present in any company, and Socrates to say, "Follow me, and hear a lecture in philosophy"; and Charles, laying his hand on his sword, to say, "Follow me and dethrone the Czar"; a man would be ashamed to follow Socrates.'

ON THE THEORY THAT WAR IS A GOOD THING FOR THE VIRTUES IT OCCASIONS

A fire might as well be thought a good thing – there is the bravery and address of the firemen employed in extinguishing it. There is much humanity exerted in saving the lives and properties of the poor sufferers. Yet after all this who can say a fire is a good thing?

SAILORS

'No man will be a sailor who has contrivance enough to get himself into a jail; for being in a ship is being in a jail, with the chance of being drowned.'

A SHIP

'A ship is worse than a jail. There is, in a jail, better air, better company, better conveniency of every kind; and a ship has the additional disadvantage of being in danger. When men come to like a sea-life, they are not fit to live on land.'

SCULPTORS

'Painting consumes labour not disproportionate to its effect; but a fellow will hack half a year at a block of marble, to make something in stone that hardly resembles a man. The value of statuary is owing to its difficulty. You would not value the finest head cut upon a carrot.'

ACTORS

'What, Sir, a fellow who claps a hump on his back, and a lump on his leg, and cries, "I am *Richard the Third*"? Nay, Sir, a ballad-singer is a higher man, for he does two things; he repeats and he sings: there is both recitation and music in his performance; the player only recites.'

LIKE DANCING DOGS

'Players, Sir! I look on them as no better than creatures set upon tables and joint stools to make faces and produce laughter, like dancing dogs.' 'But, Sir, you will allow that some players are better than others?' Johnson. 'Yes, Sir, as some dogs dance better than others.'

CIRCUS RIDERS

'Such a man, Sir, should be encouraged; for his performances show the extent of the human powers in one instance, and thus tend to raise our opinion of the faculties of man. He shows what may be attained by persevering application; so that every man may hope, that by giving as much application, although perhaps he may never ride three horses at a time, or dance upon a wire, yet he may be equally expert in whatever profession he has chosen to pursue.'

THE CHURCH

Sir, the life of a parson, of a conscientious clergyman, is not easy. I have always considered a clergyman as a father of a larger family than he is able to maintain. I would rather have Chancery suits on my hands than the cure of souls. No, Sir, I do not envy a clergyman's life as an easy one, nor do I envy the clergyman who makes it an easy life.

BISHOPS
'No man can now be made a bishop for learning and piety.'

BISHOPS AND TAVERNS
'A bishop has nothing to do at a tippling-house. It is not, indeed, immoral in him to go to a tavern; neither would it be immoral in him to whip a top in Grosvenor Square: but, if he did, I hope the boys would fall upon him, and apply the whip to *him*. There are gradations in conduct; there is morality – decency – propriety. None of these should be violated by a bishop. A bishop should not go to a house where he may meet a young fellow leading out a wench.'

CLERGY AND LEVITY
'This merriment of parsons is mighty offensive.'

BARCLAY AND PERKINS BREWERY*
'We are not here to sell a parcel of boilers and vats, but the potentiality of growing rich beyond the dreams of avarice.'

ADVICE TO MR. BARCLAY ON JOINING MR. PERKINS
Sir, a mere literary man is a dull man, a man who is solely a man of business is a selfish man, but when literature and commerce are united they make a respectable man.

A MODERN TENDENCY IN FINANCIERS
'Patriotism is the last refuge of a scoundrel.'

FINANCIAL MAGNATES
I regretted the decay of respect for men of family, and that a Nabob now would carry an election from them. *Johnson*. 'Why,

* Barclay and Perkins: Robert Barclay and John Perkins became the owners of the brewery formerly owned by Henry Thrale, husband of Hester, whose anecdotes of Johnson are one source of this collection.

Sir, the Nabob will carry it by means of his wealth, as in a country where money is highly valued, as it must be where nothing can be had without money; but if it comes to personal preference, the man of family will always carry it. There is generally a *scoundrelism* about a low man.'

TRADE AND RANK

Being asked by a young nobleman what was become of the gallantry and military spirit of the old English nobility, he replied, 'Why, my Lord, I'll tell you what has become of it: it is gone into the city to look for a fortune.'

THE NEW RICH

'Sir, they have lost the civility of tradesmen, without acquiring the manners of gentlemen.'

ON A CERTAIN JEALOUSY OF RICH TRADERS

'Why, Sir, the reason is (though I don't undertake to prove that there is a reason), we see no qualities in trade that should entitle a man to superiority. We are not angry at a soldier's getting riches, because we see that he possesses qualities which we have not. If a man returns from a battle, having lost one hand, and with the other full of gold, we feel that he deserves the gold; but we cannot think that a fellow, by sitting all day at a desk, is entitled to get above us.'

FAMILY TIES

'Sir, in a country so commercial as ours, where every man can do for himself, there is not so much occasion for that attachment. No man is thought the worse of here whose brother was hanged. In uncommercial countries, many of the branches of a family must depend on the stock; so, in order to make the head of a family take care of them, they are represented as connected with his reputation, that, self-love being interested, he may exert himself to promote their interest. You have first large circles, or clans; as commerce increases the connexion is

41

confined to families; by degrees that too goes off, as having become unnecessary, and there being few opportunities of intercourse. One brother is a merchant in the city, and another is an officer in the guards; how little intercourse can these two have.'

LEARNING AND INDUSTRY

'No, Sir. While learning to read and write is a distinction, the few who have that distinction may be the less inclined to work; but when everybody learns to read and write, it is no longer a distinction. A man who has a laced waistcoat is too fine a man to work; but if everybody had laced waistcoats, we should have people working in laced waistcoats. There are no people whatever more industrious, none who work more, than our manufacturers; yet they have all learnt to read and write. Sir, you must not neglect doing a thing immediately good, from fear of remote evil; – from fear of its being abused. A man who has candles may sit up too late, which he would not do if he had not candles; but nobody will deny that the art of making candles, by which light is continued to us beyond the time that the sun gives us light, is a valuable art, and ought to be preserved.'

GAMBLING

Johnson. 'Nay, gentlemen, let us not aggravate the matter. It is not roguery to play with a man who is ignorant of the game, while you are master of it, and so win his money; for he thinks he can play better than you, as you think you can play better than he; and the superior skill carries it.'

Erskine. 'He is a fool, but you are not a rogue.'

Johnson. 'That's much about the truth, Sir. It must be considered, that a man who only does what everyone of the society to which he belongs would do, is not a dishonest man. In the republic of Sparta, it was agreed, that stealing was not dishonourable, if not discovered. I do not commend a society where there is an agreement that what would not otherwise be fair, shall be fair; but I maintain that an individual of any society, who practises what is allowed, is not a dishonest man.'

Boswell. 'So then, Sir, you do not think ill of a man who wins, perhaps, forty thousand pounds in a winter?'

Johnson. 'Sir, I do not call a gamester a dishonest man; but I call him an unsocial man, an unprofitable man. Gaming is a mode of transferring property without producing any intermediate good. Trade gives employment to numbers, and so produces intermediate good.'

THE GAMBLER

'He is ruining himself without pleasure. A man who loses at play, or who runs out his fortune at court, makes his estate less, in hopes of making it bigger: (I am sure of this word, which was often used by him) but it is a sad thing to pass through the quagmire of parsimony, to the gulf of ruin. To pass over the flowery path of extravagance is very well.'

THE PRIZE-RING

'I am sorry that prize fighting has gone out. Every art should be preserved, and the art of defence is surely important.'

BARGAINS

A bargain is a wager of skill between man and man.

ROOM FOR KINDNESS

'Getting money is not all a man's business: to cultivate kindness is a valuable part of the business of life.'

LEISURE

'No man is obliged to do as much as he can do. A man is to have part of his life to himself. If a soldier has fought a good many campaigns, he is not to be blamed if he retires to ease and tranquillity.'

GENEROSITY
'It is better to *live* rich than to *die* rich.'

VERSATILITY
'Sir, a man may be so much of everything, that he is nothing of any thing.'

WHAT MIGHT HAVE BEEN
He observed, 'it was a most mortifying reflection for any man to consider, *what he had done,* compared with *what he might have done.*'

CONSOLATION
'There is no being so poor and so contemptible who does not think there is somebody still poorer, and still more contemptible.'

ON RETIRING
Sir, it is civil suicide.

WISH. THE FATHER
There lurks perhaps in every human heart a desire of distinction which inclines every man first to hope and then to believe that nature has given him something peculiar to himself.

Friendship

POLITENESS
Politeness is fictitious benevolence. It supplies the place of it amongst those who see each other only in publick, or but little.

READY-MADE FRIENDS
'Every man who comes into the world has need of friends. If he has to get them for himself, half his life is spent before his merit is known. Relations are a man's ready friends who support him. When a man is in real distress, he flies into the arms of his relations.'

TWO COLLEGE FRIENDS
Ay! here I used to play at draughts with Phil Jones and Fludyer. Jones loved beer and did not get very forward in the church. Fludyer turned out a scoundrel, a Whig, and said he was ashamed of having been bred at Oxford. He had a living at Putney and got under the eye of some retainers to the Court at that time, and so became a violent Whig, but he had been a scoundrel all along to be sure.

Boswell. 'Was he a scoundrel in any other way than that of being a political scoundrel? Did he cheat at draughts?'

Johnson. 'Sir, we never played for money.'

YOUTH
'Sir, I love the acquaintance of young people; because, in the first place, I don't like to think myself growing old. In the next place, young acquaintances must last longest, if they do last; and then, Sir, young men have more virtue than old men; they

have more generous sentiments in every respect. I love the young dogs of this age, they have more wit and humour and knowledge of life than we had; but then the dogs are not so good scholars. Sir, in my early years I read very hard. It is a sad reflection, but a true one, that I knew almost as much at eighteen as I do now.'

IN CONSTANT REPAIR
'If a man does not make new acquaintance as he advances through life, he will soon find himself left alone. A man, Sir, should keep his friendship *in constant repair*.'

'A LOST DAY'
'Sir, I look upon every day to be lost in which I do not make a new acquaintance.'

THE DISTRESSES OF OTHERS
Johnson. 'Why, Sir, there is much noise made about it, but it is greatly exaggerated. No, Sir, we have a certain degree of feeling to prompt us to do good; more than that, Providence does not intend. It would be misery to no purpose.'

Boswell. 'But suppose now, Sir, that one of your intimate friends was apprehended for an offence for which he might be hanged.'

Johnson. 'I should do what I could to bail him, and give him any other assistance; but if he were once fairly hanged I should not suffer.'

Boswell. 'Would you eat your dinner that day, Sir?'

Johnson. 'Yes, Sir; and eat it as if he were eating with me. Why, there's Baretti, who is to be tried for his life to-morrow, friends have risen up for him on every side; yet if he should be hanged, none of them will eat a slice of plum-pudding the less. Sir, that sympathetic feeling goes a very little way in depressing the mind.'

I told him that I had dined lately at Foote's, who shewed

me a letter which he had received from Tom Davies, telling him that he had not been able to sleep, from the concern he felt on account of *This sad affair of Baretti*, begging of him to try if he could suggest any thing that might be of service; and, at the same time, recommending to him an industrious young man who kept a pickle-shop.

Johnson. 'Ay, Sir, here you have a specimen of human sympathy; a friend hanged, and a cucumber pickled. We know not whether Baretti or the pickle-man has kept Davies from sleep: nor does he know himself. And as to his not sleeping, Sir; Tom Davies is a very great man; Tom has been upon the stage, and knows how to do those things: I have not been upon the stage, and cannot do those things.'

Boswell. 'I have often blamed myself, Sir, for not feeling for others as sensibly as many say they do.'

Johnson. 'Sir, don't be duped by them any more. You will find these very feeling people are not very ready to do you good. They *pay* you by *feeling*.'

A VITAL DILEMMA
We must either outlive our friends, or our friends must outlive us, and I see no man who would hesitate about the choice.

ON THOSE WHO PROFESS TO ACT FROM PURE BENEVOLENCE
'If there are such under the earth, or in the clouds I wish they would come up or come down. What Soame Jenyns* says upon this subject is not to be minded: he is a wit. No, Sir; to act from pure benevolence is not possible for finite beings. Human benevolence is mingled with vanity, interest, or some other motive.'

---

* Soame Jenyns: Soame Jenyns' *Free Inquiry into the Nature and Origin of Evil* argued for benevolence as the origin of human action. It provoked one of Johnson's most searching and famous reviews.

THE WIDER THE BETTER
'The more a man extends and varies his acquaintance the better.'

SOCIAL SUCCESS
'I never have sought the world; the world was not to seek me. It is rather wonderful that so much has been done for me. All the complaints which are made of the world are unjust. I never knew a man of merit neglected; it was generally by his own fault that he failed of success. A man may hide his head in a hole: he may go into the country, and publish a book now and then, which nobody reads, and then complain that he is neglected. There is no reason why any person should exert himself for a man who has written a good book: he has not written it for any individual.'

AS WE FIND THEM
In youth we are apt to be too rigorous in our expectations and to suppose that the duties of life are to be performed with unfailing exactness and regularity, but in our progress through life we are forced to abate much of our demands and to take friends such as we can find them, not as we would make them. These concessions every wise man is more ready to make to others, as he knows he shall often want them for himself, and when he remembers how often he fails in the observance of a cultivation of his best friends is willing to suppose that his friends may in their turn neglect him without any intention to offend him.

WRITING LETTERS
Do not fancy that an intermission of writing is a decay of kindness. No man is always in a disposition to write, nor has any man at all times something to say. That distrust which intrudes so often on your mind is a mode of melancholy which, if it be the business of a wise man to be happy, it is foolish to indulge; and if it be a duty to preserve our faculties entire for their proper

use it is criminal. Suspicion is very often an useless pain.

A VALETUDINARIAN

'And, Sir, he is a valetudinarian, one of those who are always mending themselves. I do not know a more disagreeable character than a valetudinarian, who thinks he may do any thing that is for his ease, and indulges himself in the grossest freedoms: Sir, he brings himself to the state of a hog in a stye.'

NEGATIVE QUALITIES

'A man will please more upon the whole by negative qualities than by positive; by never offending, than by giving a great deal of delight. In the first place, men hate more steadily than they love; and if I have said something to hurt a man once I shall not get the better of this, by saying many things to please him.'

CLIMBING

'Why, Sir, I never was near enough to great men to court them. You may be prudently attached to great men, and yet independent. You are not to do what you think wrong; and, Sir, you are to calculate, and not pay too dear for what you get. You must not give a shilling's worth of court for sixpence worth of good. But if you can get a shilling's worth of good for sixpence worth of court, you are a fool if you do not pay court.'

THE END

How can a man know where his departed friends are or whether they will be his friends in the other world? How many friendships have you known formed upon the principles of virtue? Most friendships are formed by caprice or by chance, many confederacies in vice or leagues in folly.

Conversation

FLATTERY
'Nay, Sir, flattery pleases very generally. In the first place, the flatterer may think what he says to be true: but, in the second place, whether he thinks so or not, he certainly thinks those whom he flatters of consequence enough to be flattered.'

TO THE PRAISE OF A GUSHING YOUNG LADY
'Fiddledee, my dear.'

CONVERSATION
There is in the world no real delight excepting those of sensuality but exchange of ideas in conversation, and whoever has once experienced the full flow of London talk, when he returns to country friendships and rural sports, must either be contented to turn baby again and play with the rattle or he will pine away like a great fish in a little pond and die for want of his usual food.

THE PERSONAL BIAS IN CONVERSATION
'No, Sir; every man will dispute with great good humour upon a subject in which he is not interested. I will dispute very calmly upon the probability of another man's son being hanged; but if a man zealously enforces the probability that my own son will be hanged, I shall certainly not be in a very good humour with him.'

A PLEA FOR CLIMBERS

'Why, Sir, a man is very apt to complain of the ingratitude of those who have risen far above him. A man when he gets into a higher sphere, into other habits of life, cannot keep up all his former connections. Then, Sir, those who knew him formerly upon a level with themselves, may think that they ought still to be treated as on a level, which cannot be; and an acquaintance in a former situation may bring out things which it would be very disagreeable to have mentioned before higher company, though, perhaps, everybody knows of them.'

TALES AGAINST ONESELF

'A man should be careful never to tell tales of himself to his own disadvantage. People may be amused and laugh at the time, but they will be remembered and brought out against him upon some subsequent occasion.'

SELF-DEPRECIATION

All censure of a man's self is oblique praise. It is in order to show how much he can spare. It has all the invidiousness of self-praise and all the reproach of falsehood.

CONVERSATION AS AN INTELLECTUAL TEST

Sir, it is when you come close to a man in conversation that you discover what his real abilities are. To make a speech in a public assembly is a knack. Now I honour Thurlow*, Sir, Thurlow is a fine fellow, he fairly puts his mind to yours.

QUOTATION

No, Sir, it is a good thing. Classical quotation is the parole of literary men all over the world.

---

*Thurlow: Edward Thurlow, 1st baron and Lord Chancellor, was an admirer of Johnson. Johnson was impressed by his 'vigour of mind'. (Boswell's *Life of Johnson*, ed. Hill, IV, 327n.).

THE PLEASANTEST TALK
The happiest conversation is that of which nothing is distinctly remembered but a general effect of pleasing impression.

TALKING FOR EFFECT
A man who talks for Fame can never be pleasing. The man who talks to unburden his mind is the man to delight you.

PRAISE
He who praises everybody praises nobody.

THE REAL TEST
The size of a man's understanding may always justly be measured by his mirth.

A PRECAUTION
'Let us be serious, here is a fool coming.'

A WAG
'Every man has sometime in his life an ambition to be a wag.'

THE ADVANTAGES OF RIDICULE
A man should pass a part of his time with the laughers, by which means anything ridiculous or particular about him might be presented to his view and corrected.

ON BEING INQUISITIVE
'Questioning is not the mode of conversation among gentlemen. It is assuming a superiority, and it is particularly wrong to question a man concerning himself. There may be parts of his former life which he may not wish to be made known to other persons, or even brought to his own recollection.'

VERBOSITY
A man who uses a great many words to express his meaning is like a bad marksman who instead of aiming a single stone at

an object takes up a handful and throws at it in hopes he may hit.

ON A CERTAIN M.P.
Sir, this man has a pulse in his tongue.

PRESENT PERSONALITY
'Never speak of a man in his own presence. It is always indelicate, and may be offensive.'

ON TALKING OF ONE'S AILMENTS
'Do not be like the spider, man, and spin conversation thus incessantly out of thine own bowels.'

CONVERSATIONAL INGREDIENTS
Talking of conversation he said: 'There must, in the first place, be knowledge, there must be materials; – in the second place, there must be a command of words; – in the third place, there must be imagination, to place things in such views as they are not commonly seen in; – and in the fourth place, there must be presence of mind, and a resolution that it is not to be overcome by failures; this last is an essential requisite; for want of it, many people do not excel in conversation. Now *I* want it; I throw up the game upon losing a trick.'

MR. THRALE'S CONVERSATION
Why, Sir, his conversation does not show the minute hand, but he strikes the hour very correctly.

WITS
'Sir, there is nothing by which a man exasperates most people more, than by displaying a superior ability of brilliancy in conversation. They seem pleased at the time; but their envy makes them curse him at their hearts.'

ON THE USUAL RUBBISH ABOUT INVASION
Alas, alas, how this unmeaning stuff spoils all my comfort

in my friends' conversation. Will the people never have done with it, and shall I never hear a sentence again without the French in it. There is no invasion coming and you know there is none.

A NATIONAL CHARACTERISTIC
'Sir, two men of any other nation who are shown into a room together, at a house where they are both visitors, will immediately find some conversation. But two Englishmen will probably go each to a different window, and remain in obstinate silence. Sir, we as yet do not enough understand the common rights of humanity.'

A CERTAIN DISTINCTION
'No, Sir; we had *talk* enough, but no *conversation*; there was nothing *discussed*.'

THE FRENCH
'A Frenchman must be always talking, whether he knows anything of the matter or not; an Englishman is content to say nothing, when he has nothing to say.'

CONTRADICTION AS A SOCIAL STIMULANT
'To be contradicted, in order to force you to talk, is mighty unpleasing. You *shine*, indeed; but it is by being *ground*.'

DUMB DOGS
'I remember I was once on a visit at the house of a lady for whom I had a high respect. There was a good deal of company in the room. When they were gone, I said to this lady, "What foolish talking have we had!" – "Yes (said she), but while they talked you said nothing." – I was struck with the reproof. How much better is the man who does any thing that is innocent, than he who does nothing. Besides, I love anecdotes. I fancy mankind may come, in time, to write all aphoristically, except in narrative; grow weary of preparation, and connection, and illustration, and

all those arts by which a big book is made. – If a man is to wait till he weaves anecdotes into a system, we may be long in getting them, and get but few, in comparison of what we might get.'

THE LIMITS OF EGOTISM
'A man cannot with propriety speak of himself, except he relates simple facts; as, "I was at Richmond": or what depends on mensuration; as, "I am six feet high." He is sure he has been at Richmond; he is sure he is six feet high; but he cannot be sure he is wise, or that he has any other excellence. Then, all censure of a man's self is oblique praise. It is in order to show how much he can spare. It has all the invidiousness of self-praise, and all the reproach of falsehood.'

THE GRAMMAR OF ASSENT
'Sir, your assent to a man whom you have never known to falsify, is a debt: but after you have known a man to falsify, your assent to him then is a favour.'

ON A GENTLEMAN GIVEN TO TERMINOLOGICAL INEXACTITUDE
'Suppose we believe one *half* of what he tells.'
Johnson. 'Ay; but we don't know *which* half to believe.'

AN ADVANTAGE OF BREEDING
The difference, he observed, between a well-bred and an ill-bred man is this: 'One immediately attracts your liking, the other your aversion. You love the one till you find reason to hate him: you hate the other till you find reason to love him.'

EXAGGERATION
Exaggeration and the absurdities ever faithfully attached to it are inseparable attributes of the ignorant, the empty and the affected. Hence those eloquent tropes so familiar in every conversation: Monstrously pretty. Vastly little . . . hence your eminent shoe-maker farriers and undertakers . . . It is to the

same muddy source we owe the many falsehoods and absurdities we have been pestered with concerning Lisbon. Hence your extravagantly sublime figures: Lisbon is no more, can be seen no more, etc.. . . with all the other prodigal effusions of bombast beyond the stretch of time or temper to enumerate.

TRUTH

The general rule is that truth should never be violated, because it is of the utmost importance to the comfort of life that we should have a full security by mutual faith, and occasional inconveniences should be willingly suffered that we may preserve it. There must however be some exceptions: If, for instance, a murderer should ask you which way a man is gone, you may tell him what is not true, because you are under a previous obligation not to betray a man to a murderer. *Boswell*. 'Supposing the person who wrote *Junius** were asked whether he was the author, might he deny it?' *Johnson*. 'I do not know what to say to this. If you were sure he wrote *Junius*, would you, if he denied it, think as well of him afterwards?' Yet it may be urged that what a man has no right to ask you may refuse to communicate and there is no other effective mode of preserving a secret and an important secret the discovery of which may be very hurtful to you but a flat denial, for if you are silent or hesitate or evade it will be held equivalent to a confession. But stay, Sir, here is another case. Supposing the author had told me confidentially that he had written *Junius*, and I were asked if he had, I should hold myself at liberty to deny it as being under a previous promise express or implied to conceal it. Now what I ought to do for the author may I not do for myself? But I deny the lawfulness of telling a lie to a sick man for fear of alarming him. You have no business with consequences, you are to tell

---

* *Junius*: A pseudonym for the author of the famous *Letters*, published 1769-71. Johnson attacked Junius in his 'Thoughts on the Late Transactions respecting Falkland's Islands' (1771).

the truth; besides you are not sure what effect your telling him that he is in danger may have. It may bring his distemper to a crisis and that may cure him. Of all lying I have the greatest abhorrence of this, because I believe it has been frequently practised on myself.'

CONSECRATED LIES
There are inexcusable lies and consecrated lies. For instance we are told that on the arrival of the news of the unfortunate battle of Fontenoy, every heart beat and every eye was in tears. No; we know that no man eat his dinner the worse; but there *should* have been all this concern, and to say there was may be reckoned a consecrated lie.

STORIES
A story is a specimen of human manners and derives its sole value from its truth. When Foote has told me something, I dismiss it from my mind like a passing shadow. When Reynolds* tells me something I consider myself possessed of an idea the more.

UNFAIR
Nobody has a right to put another under such a difficulty that he must either hurt the person by telling the truth or hurt himself by telling what is not true.

WAITING DINNER
'Ought six people to be kept waiting for one?' 'Why, yes, if the one will suffer more by your sitting down than the six will do by waiting.'

CIVILITY
'Sir, a man has no more right to *say* an uncivil thing, than

* Reynolds: Sir Joshua Reynolds, the famous portrait artist and friend of Johnson.

to act one; no more right to say a rude thing to another, than to knock him down.'

MANNERS
'When you have said a man of gentle manners, you have said enough.'

HIMSELF
'I think myself a very polite man.'

DR. BARNARD
He was the only man who did justice to my good breeding. I am well bred to a degree of needless scrupulosity. No man is so cautious not to interrupt another. No man thinks it so necessary to appear attentive when others are speaking. No man so steadily refuses preference to himself and so willingly bestows it on another as I do. Nobody holds so strongly as I do the necessity of ceremony, and the ill effects which follow the breach of it, yet people think me rude, but Dr. Barnard did me justice.

CONTRADICTION
'When I was ill I desired he would tell me sincerely in what he thought my life was faulty. Sir, he brought me a sheet of paper, on which he had written down several texts of Scripture, recommending Christian charity. And when I questioned him what occasion I had given for such an animadversion, all that he could say amounted to this, – that I sometimes contradicted people in conversation. Now what harm does it do to any man to be contradicted?'

A TENDENCY
'In the tumult of conversation malice is apt to grow sprightly.'

MISUNDERSTOOD

'But indeed, Sir, I look upon myself to be a man very much misunderstood. I am not an uncandid, nor am I a severe man. I sometimes say more than I mean, in jest; and people are apt to believe me serious; however, I am more candid than I was when I was younger. As I know more of mankind, I expect less of them, and am ready now to call a man a *good man*, upon easier terms than I was formerly.'

ON A CERTAIN ADVANTAGE IN TALKING TO ROYALTY

'I found his Majesty wished I should talk, and I made it my business to talk. I find it does a man good to be talked to by his Sovereign. In the first place, a man cannot be in a passion.'

Eating and Drinking

ADVICE

'A man who has been drinking wine at all freely, should never go into a new company. With those who have partaken wine with him, he may be pretty well in unison; but he will, probably, be offensive, or appear ridiculous, to other people.'

WINE

'Sir, I have no objection to a man's drinking wine, if he can do it in moderation. I found myself apt to go to excess in it, and therefore, after having been for some time without it, on account of illness, I thought it better not to return to it. Every man is to judge for himself, according to the effects which he experiences. One of the fathers tells us, he found fasting made him so peevish that he did not practise it.'

DRINKING

'Sir, I do not say it is wrong to produce self-complacency by drinking; I only deny that it improves the mind. When I drank wine, I scorned to drink it when in company. I have drunk many a bottle by myself; in the first place, because I had need of it to raise my spirits; in the second place, because I would have nobody to witness its effects upon me.'

THE DIFFICULTY OF TEMPERANCE

'I cannot drink a little, therefore I never touch it. Abstinence is as easy to me as Temperance would be difficult.'

ITS EFFECT

'No, Sir; before dinner, men meet with great inequality of understanding; and those who are conscious of their inferiority, have the modesty not to talk. When they have drunk wine, every man feels himself happy, and loses that modesty, and grows impudent and vociferous; but he is not improved: he is only not sensible of his defects.'

WATER

'Drink water only: for you are then sure not to get drunk; whereas, if you drink wine, you are never sure.' I said drinking wine was a pleasure which I was unwilling to give up. 'Why, Sir (said he), there is no doubt that not to drink wine is a great deduction from life: but it may be necessary.' He however owned, that in his opinion a free use of wine did not shorten life; and said he would not give less for the life of a certain Scotch Lord (whom he named) celebrated for hard drinking, than for that of a sober man. 'But stay (said he, with his usual intelligence, and accuracy of inquiry), does it take much wine to make him drunk?' I answered, 'a great deal either of wine or strong punch.' 'Then (said he) that is the worse.'

SAFER

Talking of drinking wine, he said, 'I did not leave off wine, because I could not bear it! I have drunk three bottles of port without being the worse for it. University College has witnessed this.'

Boswell. 'Why then, Sir, did you leave it off?'

Johnson. 'Why, Sir, because it is so much better for a man to be sure that he is never to be intoxicated, never to lose the power over himself. I shall not begin to drink wine till I grow old and want it.'

Boswell. 'I think, Sir, you once said to me, that not to drink wine was a great deduction from life.'

Johnson. 'It is a diminution of pleasure, to be sure: but I do not say a diminution of happiness. There is more happiness in being rational.'

Boswell. 'But if we could have pleasure always, should not we be happy? The greatest part of men would compound for pleasure.'

Johnson. 'Supposing we could have pleasure always, an intellectual man would not compound for it. The greatest part of men would compound, because the greatest part of men are gross.'

Boswell. 'I allow there may be greater pleasure than from wine. I have had more pleasure from your conversation. I have indeed; I assure you I have.'

Johnson. 'When we talk of pleasure, we mean sensual pleasure. When a man says, he had pleasure with a woman, he does not mean conversation, but something of a very different nature. Philosophers tell you, that pleasure is *contrary* to happiness. Gross men prefer animal pleasure. So there are men who have preferred living among savages. Now what a wretch must he be, who is content with such conversation as can be had among savages? You may remember, an officer at Fort Augustus, who had served in America, told us of a woman whom they were obliged to *bind*, in order to get her back from savage life.'

Boswell. 'She must have been an animal, a beast.'

Johnson. 'She was a speaking cat.'

CATHEDRAL SOCIETY

'I remember (said he), when all the *decent* people in Lichfield got drunk every night, and were not the worse thought of. Ale was cheap, so you pressed strongly. When a man must bring a bottle of wine, he is not in such haste. Smoking has gone out. To be sure, it is a shocking thing blowing smoke out of our mouths, into other people's mouths, eyes, and noses, and having the same thing done to us. Yet I cannot account, why a thing which required so little exertion, and yet preserves the mind from total vacuity, should have gone out. Every man has something by which he calms himself: beating with his feet, or so. I remember when people in England changed a shirt only once a week: a Pandour, when he gets a shirt, greases it to make it last. Formerly, good tradesmen had no fire but in the kitchen; never in the parlour, except on Sunday. My father, who was a magistrate of Lichfield, lived thus. They never began to have a fire in the parlour, but on leaving off business, or some great revolution of their life.'

WINE IN SCOTLAND BEFORE THE UNION

'We had wine before the Union.'

Johnson. 'No, Sir; you had some weak stuff, the refuse of France which would not make you drunk.'

Boswell. 'I assure you, Sir, there was a great deal of drunkenness.'

Johnson. 'No, Sir; there were people who died of dropsies, which they contracted in trying to get drunk.'

TO BOSWELL THE NEXT MORNING AFTER FOUR BOWLS OF PUNCH IN SKYE

'What, drunk yet?' – His tone of voice was not that of severe upbraiding; so I was relieved a little. – 'Sir', said I, 'they kept me up.' – He answered, 'No, you kept them up, you drunken dog.'

A PASTIME

He said, few people had intellectual resource sufficient to forgo the pleasures of wine. They could not otherwise contrive how to fill the interval between dinner and supper.

THE RETORT COURTEOUS

A gentleman having to some of the usual arguments for drinking added this: 'You know Sir, drinking drives away care, and makes us forget whatever is disagreeable. Would not you allow a man to drink for that reason?'

Johnson. 'Yes, Sir, if he sat next *you*.'

IN VINO VERITAS
'Why, Sir, that may be an argument for drinking, if you suppose men in general to be liars. But, Sir, I would not keep company with a fellow who lies as long as he is sober, and whom you must make drunk before you can get a word of truth out of him.'

A CHOICE
'A man may choose whether he will have abstemiousness and knowledge, or claret and ignorance.'

PRUDENCE IN DRINKING
'Drinking may be practised with great prudence; a man who exposes himself when he is intoxicated, has not the art of getting drunk; a sober man, who happens occasionally to get drunk, readily enough goes into a new company, which a man who has been drinking should never do. Such a man will undertake any thing; he is without skill in inebriation. I used to slink home when I had drunk too much. A man accustomed to self-examination will be conscious when he is drunk, though an habitual drunkard will not be conscious of it. I knew a physician, who for twenty years was not sober; yet in a pamphlet, which he wrote upon fevers, he appealed to Garrick and me for his vindication from a charge of drunkenness. A bookseller (naming him) who got a large fortune by trade, was so habitually and equally drunk, that his most intimate friends never perceived that he was more sober at one time than another.'

THE HEADACHE
'Nay, Sir, it was not the *wine* that made your head ache, but the *sense* that I put into it.'

WHAT TO DRINK
Johnson harangued upon the qualities of different liquors, and spoke with great contempt of claret, as so weak, that 'a man would be drowned by it before it made him drunk.' He was

persuaded to drink one glass of it, that he might judge, not from recollection, which might be dim, but from immediate sensation. He shook his head, and said, 'Poor stuff! No, Sir; claret is the liquor for boys; port for men; but he who aspires to be a hero (smiling) must drink brandy. In the first place, the flavour of brandy is most grateful to the palate, and then brandy will do soonest for a man what drinking *can* do for him. There are, indeed, few who are able to drink brandy. That is a power rather to be wished for than attained. And yet (proceeded he), as in all pleasure hope is a considerable part, I know not but fruition comes too quick by brandy. Florence wine I think the worst; it is wine only to the eye; it is wine neither while you are drinking it, nor after you have drunk it; it neither pleases the taste, nor exhilarates the spirits.'

ON MRS. WILLIAMS* WONDERING WHY MEN MADE BEASTS OF THEMSELVES

I wonder, Madam, that you have not penetration enough to see the strong inducement to this excess, for he who makes a beast of himself gets rid of the pain of being a man.

'CONDITIONS OF LIFE'

Every man is to take existence on the terms on which it is given to him. To some men it is given on condition of not taking liberties, which other men may take without much harm. One may drink wine, and be nothing the worse for it; on another, wine may have effects so inflammatory as to injure him both in body and mind, and perhaps make him commit something for which he may deserve to be hanged.

ON DINING WITH A DUKE

'To be sure, Sir, if you were to dine only once, and it were never to be known where you dined, you would choose rather to dine with the first man of genius: but to gain most respect, you

---

* Mrs. Williams: Anna Williams, the friend and lodger of Johnson.

should dine with the first Duke in England. For nine people in ten that you meet with would have a higher opinion of you for having dined with a Duke; and the great genius himself would receive you better, because you had been with the great Duke.'

A FOOLISH POSE
'Some people have a foolish way of not minding, or pretending not to mind, what they eat. For my part, I mind my belly very studiously, and very carefully; for I look upon it, that he who does not mind his belly will hardly mind anything else.'

AN INFALLIBLE TEST
Whenever the dinner is ill got, there is poverty, or there is avarice, or there is stupidity. In short the family is somehow grossly wrong.

A DIFFERENCE SOMETIMES FORGOTTEN
'This was a good dinner enough, to be sure; but it was not a dinner to *ask* a man to.'

A GOOD DINNER
'Sir, we could not have had a better dinner had there been a *Synod of Cooks*.'

ON CARRYING LEMONS TO SKYE 'THAT HE MIGHT BE SURE OF HIS LEMONADE'
'Sir, I do not wish to be thought that feeble man who cannot do without anything. Sir, it is very bad manners to carry provisions to any man's house, as if he could not entertain you. To an inferiour, it is oppressive; to a superiour, it is insolent.'

DIET
I never felt any difference upon myself from eating one thing rather than another. There are people I believe who feel a difference, but I am not one of them; and as to regular meals, I have fasted from the Sunday's dinner to the Tuesday's dinner without any inconvenience. I believe it best to eat just as one is

hungry, but a man who is in business, or a man who has a family must have stated meals.

APPETITE
Sir, a man who rides out for appetite consults but little the dignity of human nature.

ORCHARDS
He advised me, if possible, to have a good orchard. He knew, he said, a clergyman of small income, who brought up a family very reputably, which he chiefly fed with apple-dumplings.

HOSPITALITY
'It will never do, Sir. There is nothing served about there, neither tea, nor coffee, nor lemonade, nor anything whatever; and depend upon it, Sir, a man does not love to go to a place from whence he comes out exactly as he went in.'

ON BEING REMINDED BY SIR JOSHUA REYNOLDS THAT HE DRANK ELEVEN CUPS OF TEA
Sir, I did not count your glasses of wine, why should you number up my cups of tea? Sir, I should have released the lady from any further trouble had it not been for your remark, but you have reminded me that I want one of the dozen and I must request Mrs. Cumberland to round up my number.

ON BEING ASKED BY LADY MACLEOD AFTER SIXTEEN CUPS WHETHER HE WOULD NOT PREFER A SMALL BASIN
I wonder, Madam, why all the ladies ask me such questions. It is to save yourselves trouble and not me.

A CERTAIN JOINT OF ROAST MUTTON
'It is as bad as bad can be: it is ill-fed, ill-killed, ill-kept, and ill-drest.'

ON DINING WITH LORD MONBODDO 'WHO AFFECTS AN
ABSTEMIOUS SYSTEM'
'I have done greater feats with my knife than this.'

THE OBJECT OF DINNER-PARTIES

'Why, to eat and drink together, and to promote kindness;
and, Sir, this is better done where there is no solid conversation;
for, when there is, people differ in opinion, and get into bad
humour; or some of the company, who are not capable of such
conversation, are left out, and feel themselves uneasy. It was for
this reason, Sir Robert Walpole said, he always talked bawdy at
his table, because in that all could join.'

DINNER

I never but once upon a resolution to employ myself in
study balked an invitation out to dinner, and then I stayed at
home and did nothing.

GOOD THINGS

'Sir, when a man is invited to dinner, he is disappointed if
he does not get something good. I advised Mrs. Thrale, who has
no card-parties at her house, to give sweetmeats, and such good
things, in an evening, as are not commonly given, and she would
find company enough come to her: for everybody loves to have
things which please the palate put in their way, without trouble
or preparation.'

LIVING IN FRANCE

'The great in France live very magnificently, but the rest
very miserably. There is no happy middle state, as in England.
The shops of Paris are mean: the meat in the markets is such as
would be sent to a gaol in England; and Mr. Thrale justly
observed, that the cookery of the French was forced upon them
by necessity; for they could not eat their meat, unless they added
some taste to it. The French are an indelicate people; they will
spit upon any place. At Madame ———'s, a literary lady of

rank, the footman took the sugar in his fingers, and threw it into my coffee. I was going to put it aside; but hearing it was made on purpose for me, I e'en tasted Tom's fingers. The same lady would needs make tea à l'Angloise. The spout of the tea-pot did not pour freely; she bade the footman blow into it. France is worse than Scotland in everything but climate. Nature has done more for the French; but they have done less for themselves than the Scotch have done.'

TAVERNS

'There is no private house in which people can enjoy themselves so well as in a capital tavern. Let there be ever so great plenty of good things, ever so much grandeur, ever so much elegance, ever so much desire that everybody should be easy; in the nature of things it cannot be: there must always be some degree of care and anxiety. The master of the house is anxious to entertain his guests; the guests are anxious to be agreeable to him: and no man, but a very impudent dog indeed, can as freely command what is in another man's house, as if it were his own. Whereas, at a tavern, there is a general freedom from anxiety. You are sure you are welcome: and the more noise you make, the more trouble you give, the more good things you call for, the welcomer you are. No servants will attend you with the alacrity which waiters do, who are incited by the prospect of an immediate reward in proportion as they please. No, Sir; there is nothing which has yet been contrived by man, by which so much happiness is produced as by a good tavern or inn.'

'THEIR CHARM'

'As soon as I enter the door of a tavern, I experience an oblivion of care, and of freedom from solicitude: when I am seated, I find the master courteous, and the servants obsequious to my call; anxious to know and ready to supply my wants; wine there exhilarates my spirits, and prompts me to free conversation and an interchange of discourse with those whom I most love: I dogmatise and am contradicted, and in this conflict of opinion and sentiments I find delight.'

'FELICITY'
'A tavern chair is the throne of human felicity.'

COOKING AND PHILOSOPHY

I could write a better book of cookery than has ever yet been written; it should be a book upon philosophical principles. Pharmacy is now made much more simple, cookery may be made so too. A prescription which is now composed of five ingredients, had formerly fifty in it. So in cookery, if the nature of the ingredients be well known, much fewer will do.

Then, as you cannot make bad meat good, I would tell what is the best butcher's meat, the best beef, the best pieces, how to choose young fowls. The proper season of different vegetables and then how to roast and boil and compound.

Dilly. Mrs. Glasse's Cookery, which is the best, was written by Dr. Hill; half the trade know this.

Johnson. Well, Sir, this shows how much better the subject of cookery may be treated by a philosopher. I doubt if the book be written by Dr. Hill, for in Mrs. Glasse's Cookery, which I have looked into, saltpetre and salprunella are spoken of as different substances, whereas salprunella is only saltpetre burnt on charcoal and Hill could not be ignorant of this. However, as the greatest part of such a book is made by transcription, this mistake may have been carelessly adopted, but you shall see what a book of cookery I shall make. I shall agree with Mr. Dilly for the copyright.

Miss Seward. That would be Hercules with the distaff indeed.

Johnson. No, Madam. Women can spin very well but they cannot make a good book of cookery.

Happiness

THE PRESENT
He asserted, that *the present* was never a happy state to any human being; but that, as every part of life, of which we are conscious, was at some point of time a period yet to come, in which felicity was expected, there was some happiness produced by hope. Being pressed upon this subject, and asked if he really was of opinion, that though, in general, happiness was very rare in human life, a man was not sometimes happy in the moment that was present, he answered, 'Never, but when he is drunk.'

RANELAGH*
'Alas, Sir, these are all only struggles for happiness. When I first entered Ranelagh, it gave an expansion and gay sensation to my mind, such as I never experienced anywhere else. But, as Xerxes wept when he viewed his immense army, and considered that not one of that great multitude would be alive a hundred years afterwards, so it went to my heart to consider that there was not one in all that brilliant circle, that was not afraid to go home and think; but that the thoughts of each individual there would be distressing when alone.'

THE HAPPY MAN
'It's all cant; the dog knows he is miserable all the time.'

* Ranelagh: At Chelsea, a frequent resort of Johnson.

DEGREES OF HAPPINESS
'Sir, that all who are happy, are equally happy, is not true. A peasant and a philosopher may be equally *satisfied*, but not equally *happy*. Happiness consists in the multiplicity of agreeable consciousness. A peasant has not capacity for having equal happiness with a philosopher.'

OBLIVION
'That man is never happy for the present, is so true, that all his relief from unhappiness is only forgetting himself for a little while. Life is a progress from want to want, not from enjoyment to enjoyment.'

SORROW
Sorrow is the rust of the soul; activity will cleanse and brighten it.

THE DURATION OF GRIEF
'All grief for what cannot in the course of nature be helped soon wears away; in some sooner indeed, in some later; but it never continues very long, unless where there is madness, such as will make a man have pride so fixed in his mind, as to imagine himself a king; or any other passion in an unreasonable way: for all unnecessary grief is unwise, and therefore will not long be retained by a sound mind. If, indeed, the cause of our grief is occasioned by our own misconduct, if grief is mingled with remorse of conscience, it should be lasting.'

WITH MEN AND WOMEN
'No, Sir, Thrale will forget it first. *She* has many things that she *may* think of. *He* has many things that he *must* think of.'

CONSOLATION
'While grief is fresh, every attempt to divert only irritates. You must wait till grief be *digested*, and then amusement will dissipate the remains of it.'

ON A LADY WHO DIED OF GRIEF FOR HER HUSBAND

She was rich and wanted employment so she cried until she lost all power of restraining her tears. Other women are forced to outlive their husbands who were just as much beloved, depend upon it, but they have no time for grief, and I doubt not if we had put my Lady Tavistock into a small chandler's shop and given her a nurse child to tend, her life would have been saved. The poor and the busy have no leisure for sentimental sorrow.

A SAFE INFERENCE

Depend upon it that if a man talks of his misfortunes there is something in them that is not disagreeable to him, for where there is nothing but pure misery, there never is any recourse to the mention of it.

EXCESSIVE VIRTUE

Beware of romantic virtue. It is founded on no settled principle. A plank that is tilted up at one end must of course fall down on the other.

PITY

'Pity is not natural to man. Children are always cruel. Savages are always cruel. Pity is acquired and improved by the cultivation of reason. We may have uneasy sensations from seeing a creature in distress, without pity; for we have not pity unless we wish to relieve them. When I am on my way to dine with a friend, and finding it late, have bid the coachman make haste, if I happen to attend when he whips his horses, I may feel unpleasantly that the animals are put to pain, but I do not wish him to desist. No, Sir, I wish him to drive on.'

AFFECTATION

Sir, it is affectation to pretend to feel the distress of others, as much as they do themselves. It is as if one should pretend to feel as much pain when a friend's leg is cutting off as he does.

HARDNESS

Want of tenderness is want of parts, and is no less a proof of stupidity than depravity.

FEAR

'Fear is one of the passions of human nature, of which it is impossible to divest it. You remember that the Emperor Charles V, when he read upon the tombstone of a Spanish nobleman, "Here lies one who never knew fear," wittily said: "Then he never snuffed a candle with his fingers." '

THE INFLUENCE OF CLIMATE ON HAPPINESS

'Nay, Sir, how can you talk so? What is *climate* to happiness? place me in the heart of Asia, should I not be exiled? What proportion does climate bear to the complex system of human life? You may advise me to go to live at Bologna to eat sausages. The sausages there are the best in the world; they lose much by being carried.'

FINE AIR

Sir, this is all imagination which physicians encourage, for man lives in air as a fish lives in water, so that if the atmosphere presses heavy from above, there is an equal resistance from below.

HAPPINESS AND WEATHER

'Surely, nothing is more reproachful to a being endowed with reason, than to resign its powers to the influence of the air, and live in dependance on the weather and the wind for the only blessings which nature has put into our power, tranquillity and benevolence. This distinction of seasons is produced only by imagination operating on luxury. To temperance, every day is bright; and every hour is propitious to diligence. He that shall resolutely excite his faculties, or exert his virtues, will soon make himself superior to the seasons; and may set at defiance the morning mist and the evening damp, the blasts of the east, and the clouds of the south.'

SOLITUDE

Solitude is dangerous to reason without being favourable to virtue, pleasures of some sort are necessary to the intellectual as to the corporeal health, and those who resist gaiety will be likely for the most part to fall a sacrifice to appetite, for the solicitations of sense are always at hand and a dram to a vacant and solitary person is a speedy and seducing relief. Remember the solitary mortal is certainly luxurious, probably superstitious, and possibly mad. The mind stagnates for want of employment, grows morbid, and is extinguished like a candle in foul air.

MELANCHOLY

Some men and many thinking men have not these vexing thoughts. Sir Joshua Reynolds is the same all the year round. Beauclerk except when ill and in pain is the same, but I believe most men have them in the degree in which they are capable of having them. If I were in the country and distressed by that malady I would force myself to take a book, and every time I did it I should find it the easier. Melancholy indeed should be diverted by every means except by drinking.

ITS TREATMENT

A man so afflicted, Sir, must divert distressing thoughts and not combat with them.

Boswell. 'May he not think them down, Sir?'

Johnson. 'No, Sir, to attempt to think them down is madness. He should have a lamp constantly burning in his bed-chamber during the night, and if wakefully disturbed take a book and read and compose himself to rest. To have the management of his mind is a great art, and it may be obtained in a considerable degree by experience and habitual exercise.'

Boswell. 'Should he not provide amusement for himself? Would it not be right for instance for him to take a course of chemistry?'

    Johnson. 'Let him take a course of chemistry or a course of rope-dancing or a course of anything to which he is inclined at the time. Let him contrive to have as many retreats for the mind as he can, as many things to which it can fly from itself.'

SILENCE

    When any fit of anxiety or gloominess or perversion of the mind lays hold upon you make it a rule not to publish it by complaints but exert your whole care to hide it. By endeavouring to hide it you will drive it away. Be always busy.

MITIGATION

    There is nothing too little for so little a creature as man. It is by studying little things that we attain the great art of having as little misery and as much happiness as possible.

London

FOR LITERARY MEN
No man, fond of letters, leaves London without regret.

THE INTELLIGENT AND THE THRIFTY
'London is nothing to some people; but to a man whose pleasure is intellectual, London is the place. And there is no place where economy can be so well practised as in London: more can be had here for the money, even by ladies, than anywhere else. You cannot play tricks with your fortune in a small place; you must make an uniform appearance. Here a lady may have well- furnished apartments, and elegant dress, without any meat in her kitchen.'

ITS POSSIBILITIES
'The happiness of London is not to be conceived but by those who have been in it. I will venture to say, there is more learning and science within the circumference of ten miles from where we now sit, than in all the rest of the kingdom.'

ITS IMMENSITY
'Sir, if you wish to have a just notion of the magnitude of this city, you must not be satisfied with seeing its great streets and squares, but must survey the innumerable little lanes and courts. It is not in the showy evolutions of buildings, but in the multiplicity of human habitations, which are crowded together, that the wonderful immensity of London consists.'

AS A RESORT FOR THE VAIN AND THE SUSCEPTIBLE

No place cures a man's vanity or arrogance, so well as London; for as no man was either great or good *per se*, but as compared with others not so good or great, he is sure to find in the metropolis many his equals, and some his superiors. A man in London is in less danger of falling in love indiscreetly, than anywhere else; for there the difficulty of deciding between the conflicting pretensions of a vast variety of objects, keep him safe.

ITS HUB

'Why, Sir, Fleet Street has a very animated appearance; but I think the full tide of human existence is at Charing Cross.'

AS A PERMANENT RESIDENCE

'Why, Sir, you find no man, at all intellectual, who is willing to leave London. No, Sir, when a man is tired of London, he is tired of life; for there is in London all that life can afford.'

AS A HELP TO RURAL DOMESTICITY

'A country gentleman should bring his lady to visit London as soon as he can, that they may have agreeable topics for conversation when they are by themselves.'

THE ONLY EXCUSE FOR COUNTRY LIFE

'No wise man will go to live in the country, unless he has something to do which can be better done in the country. For instance: if he is to shut himself up for a year to study a science, it is better to look out to the fields, than to an opposite wall. Then, if a man walks out in the country, there is nobody to keep him from walking in again; but if a man walks out in London, he is not sure when he shall walk in again. A great city is, to be sure, the school for studying life; and "The proper study of mankind is man," as Pope observes.'

BOEOTIANS

'Sir, it is in the intellectual world as in the physical world:

we are told by natural philosophers that a body is at rest in the place that is fit for it; they who are content to live in the country, are *fit* for the country.'

STAGNATION
'Country gentlemen must be unhappy for they have not enough to keep their lives in motion.'

BOSWELL AMD LONDON
'Why, Sir, I never knew any one who had such a gust for London as you have, and I cannot blame you for your wish to live there. Yet, Sir, were I in your father's place I should not consent to your settling there, for I have the old feudal notions and I should be afraid that Auchinleck would be deserted, as you would soon find it more desirable to have a country seat in a better climate. I own, however, to consider it a duty to reside on a family estate is a prejudice, for we must consider that working people get employment equally and the produce of the land is sold equally, whether a great family resides at home or not, and if the rents of an estate be carried to London they return again in the circulation of commerce. Nay, Sir, we must perhaps allow that carrying the rents to a distance is good because it contributes to the circulation. We must, however, allow that a well-regulated great family may improve a neighbourhood in civility and elegance and give an example of good order, virtue, and piety, and so its residence at home may be of much advantage; but if a great family be disorderly and vicious, its residence at home is very pernicious to a neighbourhood. There is not now the same inducement to live in the country as formerly, the pleasures of social life are much better enjoyed in town and there is no longer in the country that power and influence in proprietors of land which they had in the old times and which made the country so agreeable to them. The Laird of Auchinleck now is not near so great a man as the Laird of Auchinleck was a hundred years ago.'

THE WALL

In the last age, when my mother lived in London, there were two sets of people, those who gave the wall and those who took it: the peaceable and the quarrelsome. When I returned to Lichfield, after having been in London, my mother asked me whether I was one of those who gave the wall, or who took it. Now it is fixed that every man keeps to the right, or if one is taking the wall another gives it and it is never a dispute.

Scotland, Ireland, and the Americans

SCOTLAND
There can never be a good map of Scotland. Why, Sir, to measure land a man must go over it, but who would think of going over Scotland?

EXPLAINED
That is a very vile country to be sure, Sir. 'Well, Sir, God made it.' Certainly He did, but we must always remember He made it for Scotchmen.

THEIR LEARNING
'Their learning is like bread in a besieged town: every man gets a little, but no man gets a full meal.' 'There is in Scotland a diffusion of learning, a certain portion of it widely and thinly spread. A merchant has as much learning as one of their clergy.'

THEIR NATIONAL BIAS
He also was outrageous, upon his supposition that my countrymen 'loved Scotland better than truth,' saying, 'All of them, – nay not all, – but *droves* of them, would come up, and attest any thing for the honour of Scotland.'

WHEN
'When I find a Scotchman, to whom an Englishman is as a Scotchman, that Scotchman shall be as an Englishman to me.'

THEIR EDUCATION
'As an Englishman, I should wish all the Scotch gentlemen

should be educated in England; Scotland would become a province; they would spend all their rents in England.'

THEIR WAY
'One of that nation who had been a candidate, against whom I had voted, came up to me with a civil salutation. Now, Sir, this is their way. An Englishman would have stomached it, and been sulky, and never have taken farther notice of you; but a Scotchman, Sir, though you vote nineteen times against him, will accost you with equal complaisance after each time, and the twentieth time, Sir, he will get your vote.'

SCOTLAND
'Seeing Scotland, Madam, is only seeing a worse England. It is seeing the flower gradually fade away to the naked stalk. Seeing the Hebrides, indeed, is seeing quite a different scene.'

ITS NOBLEST PROSPECT
'But, Sir, let me tell you, the noblest prospect which a Scotchman ever sees, is the high road that leads him to England!'

BOSWELL AND HIS EXCUSE
'I do indeed, come from Scotland, but I cannot help it.'
'That, Sir, I find, is what a very great many of your countrymen cannot help.'

ALSO
Nay, Sir, I do value you more by being a Scotchman. You are a Scotchman without the faults of Scotchmen. You would not have been as valuable as you are had you not been a Scotchman.

WHISKY
'Come let me know what it is that makes a Scotchman happy.'

SCOTLAND
'Your country consists of two things, stone and water. There is, indeed, a little earth above the stone in some places, but a very little; and the stone is always appearing. It is like a man in rags; the naked skin is still peeping out.'

THEIR CHIVALRY
'Sir, never talk of your independency, who could let your Queen remain twenty years in captivity, and then be put to death, without even a pretence of justice, without your ever attempting to rescue her; and such a Queen too! as every man of any gallantry of spirit would have sacrificed his life for.'

THE HIGHLANDS
'How, Sir, can you ask me what obliges me to speak unfavourably of a country where I have been hospitably entertained? Who *can* like the Highlands? – I like the inhabitants very well.'

'ON THE SCOTCH ABOLISHING VAILS'
Sir, you were too poor to give them.

HOW THE DELUSION AROSE THAT A STRANGER LANDING IN ST. KILDA GIVES THE NATIVES A COLD
'The steward always comes to demand something from them; and so they fall a coughing.'

THEIR BENEVOLENCE
'While they confine their benevolence in a manner, exclusively to those of their own country, they expect to share in the good offices of other people. Now this principle is either right or wrong; if right, we should do well to imitate such conduct; if wrong, we cannot too much detest it.'

THE ONLY CHANCE
'Much may be made of a Scotchman, if he be *caught* young.'

THE RUB

'Sir, it is not so much to be lamented that Old England is lost, as that the Scotch have found it.'

IRELAND AND HOME RULE

On the subject of an Union which artful Politicians have often had in view – 'Do not make an union with us, Sir; we should unite with you, only to rob you. We should have robbed the Scotch, if they had anything of which we could have robbed them.'

IRELAND

Before dinner, he told us of a curious conversation between the famous George Faulkner and him. George said that England had drained Ireland of fifty thousand pounds in specie, annually, for fifty years. 'How so, Sir! (said Dr. Johnson) you must have a very great trade?' 'No trade.' – 'Very rich mines?' 'No mines.' – 'From whence, then, does all this money come?' 'Come! why out of the blood and bowels of the poor people of Ireland!'

THE IRISH

'The Irish are in a most unnatural state; for we see there the minority prevailing over the majority. There is no instance, even in the ten persecutions, of such severity as that which the Protestants of Ireland have exercised against the Catholics. Did we tell them we have conquered them, it would be above board: to punish them by confiscation and other penalties as rebels was monstrous injustice.'

AS COMPARED WITH THE SCOTCH

'The Irish mix better with the English than the Scotch do; their language is nearer to English; as a proof of which, they succeed very well as players, which Scotchmen do not. Then, Sir, they have not that extreme nationality which we find in the Scotch. I will do you, Boswell, the justice to say, that you are the most *unscottified* of your countrymen. You are almost the only instance of a Scotchman that I have known who did not at every other sentence bring in some other Scotchman.'

AGAIN
The impudence of an Irishman is the impudence of a fly that buzzes about you, and you put it away but it returns again and flutters and teazes you. The impudence of a Scotchman is the impudence of a leech which fixes and sucks your blood.

A FAIR PEOPLE
'Sir, you have no reason to be afraid of me. The Irish are not in a conspiracy to cheat the world by false representations of the merits of their countrymen. No, Sir; the Irish are a FAIR PEOPLE; – they never speak well of one another.'

ENGLISH RULE IN IRELAND
'Let the authority of the English government perish rather than be maintained by iniquity. Better would it be to restrain the turbulence of the natives by the authority of the sword, and to make them amenable to law and justice by an effectual and vigorous police, than to grind them to powder by all manner of disabilities and incapacities. Better to hang or drown people at once, than by an unrelenting persecution to beggar and starve them.'

AMERICANS
'Sir, they are a race of convicts, and ought to be thankful for anything we allow them short of hanging.'

HANDS ACROSS THE SEA
'I am willing to love all mankind, *except an American*:' 'Rascals – Robbers – Pirates; I'd burn and destroy them.'

Travel

The use of travelling is to regulate imagination by reality, and instead of thinking how things may be to see them as they are.

MAXIMS OF TRAVEL

'Observe these rules:

1. Turn all care out of your head as soon as you mount the chaise.

2. Do not think about frugality; your health is worth mo·e than it can cost.

3. Do not continue any day's journey to fatigue.

4. Take now and then a day's rest.

5. Get a smart sea-sickness, if you can.

6. Cast away all anxiety, and keep your mind easy.

This last direction is the principal; with an unquiet mind, neither exercise, nor diet, nor physic, can be of much use.'

ITALY AND THE MEDITERRANEAN

'A man who has not been in Italy is always conscious of an inferiority, from his not having seen what it is expected a man should see. The grand object of travelling is to see the shores of the Mediterranean. On those shores were the four great Empires of the world; the Assyrian, the Persian, the Grecian, and the Roman. – All our religion, almost all our law, almost all our arts, almost all that sets us above savages, has come to us from the shores of the Mediterranean.'

ON VISITING THE GREAT WALL OF CHINA

'Sir, by doing so you would do what would be of importance in raising your children to eminence. That would be a lustre reflected upon them from your spirit and curiosity. They would be at all times regarded as the children of a man who had gone to view the wall of China. I am serious, Sir.'

ALL THE DIFFERENCE

Boswell. 'Is not the Giant's-causeway worth seeing?'
Johnson. 'Worth seeing? Yes; but not worth going to see.'

EMIGRATION A MISTAKE

'For it spreads mankind, which weakens the defence of a nation, and lessens the comfort of living. Men, thinly scattered, make a shift, but a bad shift, without many things. A smith is ten miles off: they'll do without a nail or a staple. A taylor is far from them; they'll botch their own clothes. It is being concentrated which produces high convenience.'

A DANGER TO BE AVOIDED

'Well, I have a mind to see what is done in other places of learning. I'll go and visit the Universities abroad. I'll go to France and Italy. I'll go to Padua – and I'll mind my business. For an *Athenian* blockhead is the worst of all blockheads.'

THE RESULT

What does a man learn by travelling? Is Brandeck the better for travelling? What did Lord Charlemont learn in his travels except that there was a snake in one of the pyramids of Egypt?

SCENERY

I never heard such nonsense. A blade of grass is always a blade of grass whether in one country or another. Let us, if we do talk talk about something. Men and women are my subjects of enquiry. Let us see how these differ from those we have left behind.

The Whigs and Some Politicks

NUMBER ONE
'The first Whig was the Devil.'

'Whiggism is the negation of all principle.'

Take it upon my word and experience that when you see a Whig you see a rascal.

THEIR VIOLENCE
He was a Whig, with all the virulence and malevolence of his party.

STILL TO BE FOUND
'What! a Prig, Sir?'
Johnson. 'Worse, Madam; a Whig! But he is both.'

A GOOD HATER
Earl Bathurst was a man to my very heart's content: he hated a fool and he hated a rogue and he hated a Whig. He was a very good hater.

A PRETENCE
'Pulteney was as paltry a fellow as could be. He was a Whig, who pretended to be honest; and you know it is ridiculous for a Whig to pretend to be honest. He cannot hold it out.'

BURKE'S FAILING
'Sir, he is a cursed Whig, a bottomless Whig as they all are now.'

PARTY SPIRIT

'It is much increased by opposition. There was a violent Whig, with whom I used to contend with great eagerness. After his death I felt my Toryism much abated.'

PARTIES

'I can see that a man may do right to stick to a *party*; that is to say, he is a *Whig*, or he is a Tory, and he thinks one of those parties upon the whole the best, and that to make it prevail, it must be generally supported, though, in particulars, it may be wrong. He takes its faggot of principles, in which there are fewer rotten sticks than in the other, though some rotten sticks to be sure; and they cannot well be separated. But, to bind one's self to one man, or one set of men (who may be right to-day and wrong to-morrow), without any general preference of system, I must disapprove.'

UNIONS

'Providence has wisely ordered that the more numerous men are, the more difficult it is for them to agree in anything, and so they are governed. There is no doubt, that if the poor should reason, "We'll be the poor no longer, we'll make the rich take their turn," they could easily do it, were it not that they can't agree. So the common soldiers, though so much more numerous than their officers, are governed by them for the same reason.'

CONTROVERSY

Treating your adversary with respect, is giving him an advantage to which he is not entitled. The greatest part of men cannot judge of reasoning, and are impressed by character; so that, if you allow your adversary a respectable character, they will think, that though you differ from him, you may be in the wrong. Sir, treating your adversary with respect, is striking soft in a battle, and as to Hume – a man who has so much conceit as to tell all mankind they have been bubbled for ages and he is the wise man who sees better than they – a man who has so little scrupulosity as to venture to oppose those principles which have been thought necessary to human happiness, is he to be surprised if another man comes and laughs at him? If he is the great man he thinks himself, all this cannot hurt him. It is like throwing peas against a rock.

IF NECESSARY

When a man voluntarily engages in an important controversy he is to do all he can to lessen his antagonist, because authority from personal respect has much weight with most people and often more than reasoning. If my antagonist writes bad language I will attack him for his bad language.

Dr. Adams. 'You would not jostle a chimney sweep?'

Johnson. 'Yes, Sir, if it were necessary to jostle him down.'

PETITIONS

'This petitioning is a new mode of distressing government, and a mighty easy one. I will undertake to get petitions either against quarter guineas or half guineas, with the help of a little hot wine. There must be no yielding to encourage this. The object is not important enough. We are not to blow up half-a-dozen palaces because one cottage is burning.'

LIBERTY

'They make a rout about *universal* liberty, without considering that all that is to be valued, or indeed can be enjoyed by individuals, is *private* liberty. Political liberty is good only so far as it produces private liberty.'

THE CONDUCT OF AN ELECTION

'If I were a man of a great estate, I would drive all the rascals whom I did not like out of the country, at an election.'

BEFORE THE GLADSTONE LEAGUE

'If I were a gentleman of landed property I would turn out

all tenants who did not vote for the candidate whom I supported.'

TORY AND WHIG

'A wise Tory and a wise Whig, I believe will agree. Their rinciples are the same, though their modes of thinking are different. A high Tory makes government unintelligible: it is lost in the clouds. A violent Whig makes it unpracticable; he is for allowing so much liberty to every man, that there is not power enough to govern any man. The prejudice of the Tory is for establishment; the prejudice of the Whig is for innovation. A Tory does not wish to give more real power to Government; but that Government should have more reverence. Then they differ as to the Church. The Tory is not for giving more legal power to the Clergy, but wishes they should have a considerable influence, founded on the opinion of mankind: the Whig is for limiting and watching them with a narrow jealousy.'

A DISTRACTION

'The notion of liberty amuses the people of England, and helps to keep off the *tædium vitæ*. When a butcher tells you that *his heart bleeds for his country*, he has, in fact, no uneasy feeling.'

THE SPIRIT OF LIBERTY

Sir, that is all visionary – I would not give half a guinea to live under one form of government rather than another. It is of no moment to the happiness of an individual. Sir, the danger of the abuse of power is nothing to a private man. What Frenchman is prevented passing his life as he pleases?

Sir Adam Ferguson. 'But, Sir, in the British constitution it is surely of importance to keep up a spirit in the people so as to preserve a balance against the crown.'

Johnson. 'Sir, I perceive you are a vile Whig. Why all this childish jealousy of the power of crown. The crown has not power enough.'

FREE SPEECH

'In short, Sir, I have got no farther than this: every man has a right to utter what he thinks truth, and every other man has a right to knock him down for it. Martyrdom is the test.'

DESPOTISM

'Why, Sir, in such a government as ours, no man is appointed to an office because he is the fittest for it, nor hardly in any other government; because there are so many connexions and dependencies to be studied. A despotic prince may choose a man to an office merely because he is the fittest for it. The King of Prussia may do it.'

ON BOSWELL'S 'WISHING MUCH TO BE IN PARLIAMENT'

'Why, Sir, unless you come resolved to support any administration you would be the worse for being in Parliament, because you would be obliged to live more expensively' – (*Boswell*). 'Perhaps I should be less happy for being in Parliament. I would never sell my vote, and I should be vexed if things went wrong' – (*Johnson*). 'That's cant, Sir. It would vex you more in the house than in the gallery' – (*Boswell*). 'Have they not vexed yourself a little, Sir? Have you not been vexed by all the turbulence of this reign, and by that absurd vote of the House of Commons: That the influence of the crown has increased, is increasing, and ought to be diminished?' – (*Johnson*). 'Sir, I have never slept an hour less, nor eat an ounce less meat. I would have knocked the factious dogs on the head, to be sure; but I was not *vexed*.'

CANT

'My dear friend, clear your *mind* of cant. You may *talk* as other people do: you may say to a man, "Sir, I am your most humble servant." You are *not* his most humble servant. You may say, "These are bad times; it is a melancholy thing to be reserved to such times." You don't mind the times. You tell a man, "I am sorry you had such bad weather the last day of your journey and were so much wet." You don't care sixpence whether he is wet or dry. You may *talk* in this manner; it is a mode of talking in Society: but don't *think* foolishly.'

POLITICAL DIFFERENCES

'Why, not so much, I think, unless when they come into competition with each other. There is none when they are only common acquaintance, none when they are of different sexes. A Tory will marry into a Whig family, without any reluctance. But indeed, in a matter of much more concern than political tenets, and that is religion, men and women do not concern themselves much about difference of opinion; and ladies set no value on the moral character of men who pay their addresses to them; the greatest profligate will be as well received as the man of the greatest virtue, and this by a very good woman, by a woman who says her prayers three times a day.' Our ladies endeavoured to defend their sex from this charge; but he roared them down! 'No, no, a lady will take Jonathan Wild as readily as St. Austin, if he has three-pence more; and what is worse, her parents will give her to him. Women have a perpetual envy of our vices; they are less vicious than we, not from choice, but because we restrict them; they are the slaves of order and fashion; their virtue is of more consequence to us than our own, so far as concerns this world.'

ON THE HARM DONE BY AN IMPRUDENT PUBLICATION IN EARLY YOUTH

'No, Sir, not much. It may, perhaps, be mentioned at an election.'

SOCIALISM

'I believe, Sir, there is not; but it is better that some should be unhappy, than that none should be happy, which would be the case in a general state of equality.'

RANK AND A FEMALE REPUBLICAN

Sir, I would no more deprive a nobleman of his respect, than of his money. I consider myself as acting a part in the great system of society, and I do to others as I would have them to do to me. I would behave to a nobleman as I should expect he would behave to me, were I a nobleman, and he Sam Johnson. Sir, there is one Mrs. Macaulay in this town, a great republican. One day when I was at her house, I put on a very grave countenance, and said to her, "Madam, I am now become a convert to your way of thinking. I am convinced that all mankind are upon an equal footing; and to give you an unquestionable proof, Madam, that I am in earnest, here is a very sensible, civil, well-behaved fellow-citizen, your footman; I desire that he may be allowed to sit down and dine with us." I thus, Sir, showed her the absurdity of the levelling doctrine. She has never liked me since. Sir, your levellers wish to level down as far as themselves, but they cannot bear levelling up to themselves. They would all have some people under them; why not, then, have some people above them.'

THE HEREDITARY PRINCIPLE

'But, Sir, as subordination is very necessary for society, and contentions for superiority very dangerous, mankind, that is to say, all civilized nations, have settled it upon a plain invariable principle. A man is born to hereditary rank; or his being appointed to certain offices gives him a certain rank. Subordination tends greatly to human happiness. Were we all upon an equality, we should have no other enjoyment than mere animal pleasure.'

A MODERN FALLACY

Our desires are not the measure of equity. It were to be desired that power should be only in the hands of the merciful and riches in the possession of the generous, but the law must leave both riches and power where it finds them and must often leave riches with the covetous and power with the cruel. Convenience may be a rule in little things where no other rule has been established. But as the great end of government is to give every man his own, no inconvenience is greater than that of making right uncertain. Nor is any man more an enemy to public peace than he who fills weak heads with imaginary claims and breaks the series of civil subordination by inciting the lower classes of mankind to encroach upon the higher.

Political and Other Economy

CORN LAWS
When the corn laws were in agitation in Ireland, by which that country has been enabled not only to feed itself, but to export corn to a large amount, Sir Thomas Robinson observed, that those laws might be prejudicial to the corn-trade of England. 'Sir Thomas (said he), you talk the language of a savage: what, Sir, would you prevent any people from feeding themselves, if by any honest means they can do it?'

FREE TRADE
'Let your imports be more than your exports, and you'll never go far wrong.'

PROTECTION
'You may have a reason why two and two should make five; but they will still make but four.'

ITS ADVOCACY
'When you are declaiming, declaim, and when you are calculating, calculate.'

FREE TRADE
'It is a mistaken notion, that a vast deal of money is brought into a nation by trade. It is not so. Commodities come from commodities, but trade produces no capital accession of wealth.'

ANY PROTECTIONIST
'Sir, he was so exuberant a talker at public meetings, that the gentlemen of his country were afraid of him. No business could be done for his declamation.'

ROUND NUMBERS
Round numbers are always wrong.

WEALTH
'Life is short. The sooner that a man begins to enjoy his wealth the better.'

ADAM SMITH AS A THEORIST
'He is mistaken, Sir: a man who has never been engaged in trade himself may, undoubtedly, write well upon trade, and there is nothing which requires more to be illustrated by philosophy than trade does. As to mere wealth, that is to say, money, it is clear that one nation or one individual cannot increase its store but by making another poorer: but trade procures what is more valuable, the reciprocation of the peculiar advantages of different countries. A merchant seldom thinks but of his own particular trade. To write a good book upon it, a man must have extensive views. It is not necessary to have practised to write well upon a subject.'

THE USE OF BANKS
'A man who keeps his money has in reality more use from it than he can have by spending it.'

WEALTH AND PARADOX
'*Cæteris paribus*, he who is rich in a civilised society, must be happier than he who is poor; as riches, if properly used (and it is a man's own fault if they are not), must be productive of the highest advantages. Money, to be sure, of itself is of no use; for its only use is to part with it. Rousseau, and all those who deal in paradoxes, are led away by a childish desire of novelty. When

I was a boy I used always to choose the wrong side of a debate, because most ingenious things, that is to say, most new things, could be said upon it. Sir, there is nothing for which you may not muster up more plausible arguments than those which are urged against wealth and other external advantages. Why, now, there is stealing; why should it be thought a crime? When we consider by what unjust methods property has been often acquired, and that what was unjustly got it must be unjust to keep, where is the harm in one man's taking the property of another from him? Besides, Sir, when we consider the bad use that many people make of their property, and how much better use the thief may make of it, it may be defended as a very allowable practice. Yet, Sir, the experience of mankind has discovered stealing to be so very bad a thing that they make no scruple to hang a man for it. When I was running about this town, a very poor fellow, I was a great arguer for the advantages of poverty; but I was at the same time, very sorry to be poor. Sir, all the arguments which are brought to represent poverty as no evil, show it to be evidently a great evil. You never find people labouring to convince you that you may live very happily upon a plentiful fortune. So you hear people talking how miserable a king must be; and yet they all wish to be in his place.'

OLD AGE PENSIONS
'Where a great proportion of the people are suffered to languish in helpless misery, that country must be ill policed and wretchedly governed: a decent provision for the poor is the true test of civilisation. Gentlemen of education, he observed, were pretty much the same in all countries; the condition of the lower orders, the poor especially, was the true mark of national discrimination.'

SAVING
Speaking of economy, he remarked it was hardly worth while to save anxiously twenty pounds a year. If a man could save

to that degree, so as to enable him to assume a different rank in society then, indeed, it might answer some purpose.

ACCOUNTS

'Keeping accounts, Sir, is of no use when a man is spending his own money, and has nobody to whom he is to account. You won't eat less beef to-day because you have written down what it cost yesterday.'

SPENDING

'A man cannot make a bad use of his money, so far as regards society, if he do not hoard it; for if he either spends it or lends it out, society has the benefit. It is in general better to spend money than to give it away; for industry was more promoted by spending money than by giving it away. A man who spends his money is sure he is doing good with it: he is not sure when he gives it away. A man who spends ten thousand a year will do more good than a man who spends two thousand and gives away eight.'

A PENURIOUS ACQUAINTANCE

Sir, he is narrow, not so much from avarice as from impotence to spend his money. He cannot find in his heart to pour out a bottle of wine but he would not much care if it should sour.

DEBT

Do not accustom yourself to consider debt only as an inconvenience. You will find it a calamity. Poverty takes away so many means of doing good and produces so much inability to resist evil, both natural and moral, that it is by all virtuous means to be avoided. Consider a man whose fortune is very narrow. Whatever be his rank by birth or whatever his reputation by intellectual excellence, what good can he do, what evil can he prevent? That he cannot help the needy is evident, he has nothing to spare; but perhaps his advice and admonition may be useful. His poverty will destroy his influence: many more can find that he is poor than that he is wise, and few will reverence the understanding that is of so little advantage to its owner.

TRADE AND LEARNING

'Why, Sir, as trade is now carried on by subordinate hands, men in trade have as much leisure as others; and now learning itself is a trade. A man goes to a bookseller, and gets what he can. We have done with patronage. In the infancy of learning, we find some great man praised for it. This diffused it among others. When it becomes general, an author leaves the great, and applies to the multitude.'

Boswell. 'It is a shame that authors are not now better patronised.'

Johnson. 'No, Sir. If learning cannot support a man, if he must sit with his hands across till somebody feeds him, it is as to him a bad thing, and it is better as it is! with patronage what flattery! what falsehood !

'While man is in equilibrio, he throws truth among the multitude, and lets them take it as they please: in patronage, he must say what pleases his patron, and it is an equal chance whether that be truth or falsehood.'

Watson. 'But is not the case now, that instead of flattering one person, we flatter the age?'

Johnson. 'No, Sir. The world always lets a man tell what he thinks, his own way. I wonder, however, that so many people have written, who might have let it alone. That people should endeavour to excel in conversation, I do not wonder; because in conversation praise is instantly reverberated.'

LUXURY

Many things which are false are transmitted from book to book and gain credit in the world – one of these is the cry against the evil of luxury. Now the truth is that luxury produces much good. Take the luxury of buildings in London. Does it not produce real advantage in the convenience and elegance of accommodation and this all from the exertion of industry. People will tell you with a melancholy face that many builders are in jail. It is plain they are in jail not for building, for rents are not fallen.

A man gives half a guinea for a dish of green peas. How much gardening does this occasion, how many labourers must the competition to have such things early in the market keep in employment. You will hear it said very gravely – why was the half guinea thus spent in luxury not given to the poor? To how many might it have afforded a good meal. Alas, has it not gone to the industrious poor, whom it is better to support than the idle poor? You are much surer you are doing good when you pay money to those who work as the recompense of their labour than when you give money merely in charity. Suppose the ancient luxury of a dish of peacock's brains were to be revived, how many carcases would be left to the poor at a cheap rate – and as to the row which is made about people who are ruined by extravagance – it is no matter to the nation that some individuals suffer. When so much general productive exertion is the consequence of luxury, the nation does not care though there are debtors in jail; nay, they would not care though their debtors were there too. Depend upon it, Sir, every state of society is as luxurious as it can be. Men always take the best they can get.

BAD BARGAINS

That will not be the case if you go to a stately shop as I always do. In such a shop it is not worth their while to take a petty advantage.

In General

A SENSIBLE MAN
'This man (said he, gravely) was a very sensible man, who perfectly understood common affairs; a man of a great deal of knowledge of the world, fresh from life, not strained through books.'

A BORE
'Sir, you have but two topics, yourself and me. I am sick of both.'

ANOTHER
The fellow's dulness is elastic and all we do is but like kicking at a woolsack.

ON BEING DROPT
'Mrs. Montague has dropt me. Now, Sir, there are people whom one should like very well to drop, but would not wish to be dropped by.'

NATIONAL CHARACTER
'There is no permanent national character; it varies according to circumstances. Alexander the Great swept India: now the Turks sweep Greece.'

ON BEING HANGED – IN PARTICULAR RELATION TO DR. DODD
'Depend upon it, Sir, when a man knows he is to be hanged in a fortnight, it concentrates his mind wonderfully.'

In General

ON A SUGGESTION IT WAS UNWHOLESOME TO WORK AFTER DINNER
'Ah, Sir, don't give way to such a fancy. At one time of my life I had taken it into my head that it was not wholesome to study between breakfast and dinner.'

TO A TEDIOUS JUSTICE WHO EXPLAINED WHY HE HAD SENT FOUR MALEFACTORS TO TRANSPORTATION
'I would I had been the fifth.'

TO AN IMPERTINENT YOUNG MAN
'Pray, now, what could you give, old gentleman, to be as young and sprightly as I am?'

'Why, Sir, I think I would almost be content to be as foolish.'

AN AFFECTED AUTHOR
'No, Sir; he does not carry *me* along with him: he leaves me behind him: or rather, indeed, he sets me before him; for he makes me turn over many leaves at a time.'

ON STAGE DOORS
'I'll come no more behind your scenes, David; for the silk stockings and white bosoms of your actresses excite my amorous propensities.'

LITERARY DESCRIPTIONS
'Gravina, an Italian critic, observes that every man desires to see that of which he has read; but no man desires to read an account of what he has seen: so much does description fall short of reality. Description only excites curiosity: seeing satisfies it.'

THE DIFFERENCE
'That there was the same difference between one learned and unlearned, as between the living and the dead.'

INVERARY – THE SEAT OF THE DUKE OF ARGYLE
'What I admire here, is the total defiance of expense.'

FILIAL DISOBEDIENCE

'Once, indeed, I was disobedient; I refused to attend my
father to Uttoxeter-market. Pride was the source of that refusal,
and the remembrance of it was painful. A few years ago I desired
to atone for this fault; I went to Uttoxeter in very bad weather,
and stood for a considerable time bare-headed in the rain, on
the spot where my father's stall used to stand. In contrition I
stood, and I hope the penance was expiatory.'

'ON HEARING OF A LEARNED PIG'

'Then the pigs are a race unjustly calumniated. *Pig* has, it
seems, not been wanting to *man*, but *man* to *pig*. We do not allow
time for his education; we kill him at a year old.'

ON BEING KISSED BY A PRETTY MARRIED LADY IN SKYE

'Do it again and let us see who will tire first.'

ON BEING WICKED

'It requires great abilities to have the *power* of being very
wicked; but not to *be* very wicked. A man who has the power,
which great abilities procure him, may use it well or ill; and it
requires more abilities to use it well than to use it ill. Wickedness
is always easier than virtue; for it takes the short cut to everything. It is much easier to steal a hundred pounds than to get it
by labour, or any other way. Consider only what act of wickedness requires great abilities to commit it, when once the person
who is to do it has the power; for *there* is the distinction. It
requires great abilities to conquer an army, but none to
massacre it after it is conquered.'

IN OLD AGE

A man generally grows wickeder as he grows older – at
least he but changes the vices of youth, headstrong passion and

wild temerity for treacherous caution and a desire to cir-
cumvent. I am always on the young people's side when there is
a dispute between them and the old ones, for you have at least
a chance for virtue till age has withered its very root.

WITH PIETY
'A wicked fellow is the most pious when he takes to it. He'll
beat you all at piety.'

ON MYSTERIES
'Where secrecy or mystery begins vice and roguery are not
far off. He leads in general an ill life who stands in fear of any
man's observation.'

THE ACTION
'A man is never so moral as just after he has committed an
offence.'

FINERY
'Sir, were I to have anything fine, it should be very fine.
Were I to wear a ring, it should not be a bauble, but a stone of
great value. Were I to wear a laced or embroidered waistcoat,
it should be very rich. I had once a very rich laced waistcoat
which I wore the first night of my tragedy.'

FOPS
He said, foppery was never cured; it was the bad stamina
of the mind, which, like those of the body, were never rectified;
once a coxcomb, and always a coxcomb.

DELICACY
Delicacy does not surely consist in impossibility to be
pleased.

NOT TO BE TAKEN TOO SERIOUSLY
'Let us not be found when our Master calls us stripping the
lace off our waistcoats, but the spirit of contention from our

souls and tongues.

'Alas. A man who cannot get to heaven in a green coat will not find his way thither sooner in a grey one.'

MEN OF THE WORLD
'A man may be so much a man of the World as to be nothing in the World.'

ON FORGETTING YOUR OWN NAME
Johnson. 'Sir, that was a morbid oblivion.'

WOMEN
'Sir, a woman's preaching is like a dog's walking on his hind legs. It is not done well; but you are surprised to find it done at all.'

THEIR LIMITATIONS
Women and cows should never run.

THE WISDOM OF THE LAW
Nature has given women so much power that the Law wisely gives them little.

WOMEN AND LIBERTY
Women have all the liberty they should wish to have. We have all the labour and the danger and the women all the advantage.

We go to sea, we build houses, we do everything in short to pay our lives to women.

ON A FALLACY POPULAR AMONG WOMEN
Boswell. 'Why, Sir, do people play this trick which I observe now, when I look at your grate, putting the shovel against it to make the fire burn?'

Johnson. 'They play the trick, but it does not make the fire burn. *There* is a better (setting the poker perpendicularly up at right angles with the grate). In days of superstition they thought, as it made a cross with the bars, it would drive away the witch.'

CONDESCENSION
'There is nothing more likely to betray a man into absurdity than *condescension*; when he seems to suppose his understanding too powerful for his company.'

SITTING FOR A PORTRAIT
'Sir, among the anfractuosities of the human mind, I know not if it may not be one, that there is a superstitious reluctance to sit for a picture.'

HERESIES
To find a substitution for violated morality, he said, was the leading feature in all perversions of religion.

A BULL-DOG
'No, Sir, he is *not* well shaped; for there is not the quick transition from the thickness of the fore-part, to the *tenuity* – the thin part – behind, – which a bull-dog ought to have.'

BIG WORDS
Do not accustom yourselves to use big words for little matters.

SOME MODERN HUMORISTS
Grand nonsense is insupportable.

WHETHER A CRIMINAL SHOULD COMMIT SUICIDE TO AVOID ARREST
'Then, Sir, let him go abroad to a distant country; let him go to some place where he is *not* known. Don't let him go to the devil where he *is* known!'

CARDS
'I am sorry I have not learnt to play at cards. It is very useful in life: it generates kindness, and consolidates society.'

EARLY HOURS

Whoever thinks of going to bed before twelve is a scoundrel.

ON 'SKIPPING'

This is surely a strange advice; you may as well resolve that whatever men you happen to get acquainted with, you are to keep to them for life. A book may be good for anything; or there may be only one thing in it worth knowing: are we to read it all through? These Voyages (pointing to the three large volumes of *Voyages to the South Sea*, which were just come out), *who* will read them through? A man had better work his way before the mast than read them through; they will be eaten by rats and mice before they are read through. There can be little entertainment in such books; one set of savages is like another.'

BOOKS

No man reads long with a folio on his table. Books that you may carry to the fire and hold readily in your hand are the most useful after all.

Such form the man of general and easy reading.

PLEASURES

'Yes, Sir, no man is a hypocrite in his pleasures.'

THE DICTIONARY

Dr. Adams. 'This is a great work, Sir. How are you to see all the etymologies?'

Johnson. 'Why, Sir, here is a shelf with Junius and Skinner and others, and there is a Welsh gentleman who has published a collection of Welsh proverbs who will help me with the Welsh.'

Adams. 'But, Sir, how can you do this in three years?'

Johnson. 'I have no doubt I can do it in three years.'

Adams. 'But the French Academy, which consists of forty members, took forty years to compile their dictionary.'

Johnson. 'Sir, thus it is. This is the proportion. Let me see:

Forty times forty is sixteen hundred; as three to sixteen hundred, so is the proportion of an Englishman to a Frenchman.'

ON BOSWELL'S REGRETTING HE DID NOT GET MORE FOR THE DICTIONARY

I am sorry, too, but it was very well. The booksellers are generous, liberal-minded men.

ON BEING ASKED WHY HE DEFINED PASTERN AS THE KNEE OF A HORSE

Ignorance, Madam, pure ignorance.

ON GETTING HIS PENSION

The English language does not afford me terms adequate to my feelings on this occasion; I must have recourse to the French. I am *pénétré* with His Majesty's goodness.

TAKING IT

'Why, Sir (said he, with a hearty laugh), it is a mighty foolish noise that they make. I have accepted of a pension as a reward which has been thought due to my literary merit; and now that I have this pension, I am the same man in every respect that I have ever been; I retain the same principles. It is true that I cannot now curse (smiling) the House of Hanover; nor would it be decent for me to drink King James's health in the wine that King George gives me money to pay for. But, Sir, I think that the pleasure of cursing the House of Hanover, and drinking King James's health, are amply over-balanced by £300 a year.'

AGAIN

'I wish my pension were twice as large that they might make twice as much noise.'

EPITAPH

'The language of the country, of which a learned man was a native, is not the language fit for his epitaph, which should be in ancient and permanent language.'

A CERTAIN LATITUDE

The writer of an epitaph should not be considered as saying nothing but what is strictly true. Allowance must be made for some degree of exaggerated praise. In lapidary inscriptions a man is not upon oath.

GHOSTS

'It is wonderful that five thousand years have now elapsed since the creation of the world, and still it is undecided whether or not there has ever been an instance of the spirit of any person appearing after death. All argument is against it, but all belief is for it.'

'NOT AT HOME'

'A servant's strict regard to truth must be weakened by such a practice. A philosopher may know that it is merely a form of denial; but few servants are such nice distinguishers. If I accustom a servant to tell a lie for *me*, have I not reason to apprehend that he will tell many lies for *himself*?'

A SOPHIST

'Why, Sir, if the fellow does not think as he speaks, he is lying; and I see not what honour he can propose to himself from having the character of a liar. But if he does really think that there is no distinction between virtue and vice, why, Sir, when he leaves our houses let us count our spoons.

LORD MONBODDO WHO HAD THEORIES AS TO THE SAVAGE LIFE AND THE LANGUAGE OF APES

'But, Sir, it is as possible that Ouran-Outang does not speak, as that he speaks. However, I shall not contest the point. I should have thought it not possible to find a Monboddo; yet *he* exists.'

THE ATTENTION OF SIR ALEXANDER GORDON

But he owned to me that he was fatigued and teased by Sir Alexander's doing too much to entertain him. I said, it was all kindness.

Johnson. 'True, Sir: but sensation is sensation.'

BEGGARS AND WOMEN

He observed once, at Sir Joshua Reynolds's, that a beggar in the street will more readily ask alms from a *man*, though there should be no marks of wealth in his appearance, than from even a well-dressed *woman*; which he accounted for from the great degree of carefulness as to money that is to be found in women; saying farther upon it, that the opportunities in general that they possess of improving their condition are much fewer than men have; and adding, as he looked round the company, which consisted of men only – there is not one of us who does not think he might be richer, if he would use his endeavour.

MADNESS

'Many a man is mad in certain instances, and goes through life without having it perceived: – for example, a madness has seized a person of supposing himself obliged literally to pray continually; had the madness turned the opposite way, and the person thought it a crime ever to pray, it might not improbably have continued unobserved.'

THE WORLD

The world has always a right to be regarded.

BIOGRAPHY

'If a man is to write *A Panegyric*, he may keep vices out of sight; but if he professes to write *A Life*, he must represent it really as it was.'

EXCEPT HIS OWN

'It is rarely well executed. They only who live with a man can write his life with any genuine exactness and discrimination; and few people who have lived with a man know what to remark about him.'

A MENTAL FOIBLE
'Every man of any education would rather be called a rascal, than accused of deficiency in *the graces*.'

EDUCATION
'I do not deny, Sir, but there is some original difference in minds; but it is nothing in comparison of what is formed by education.'

SPECIALISTS
No, Sir, people are not born with a particular genius for particular employments or studies, for it would be like saying that a man could see a great way east but could not west. It is good sense applied with diligence to what was at first a mere accident and which by great application grew to be called by the generality of mankind a particular genius.

KNOWLEDGE
'All knowledge is of itself of some value. There is nothing so minute or inconsiderable that I would not rather know it than not. In the same manner, all power, of whatever sort, is of itself desirable. A man would not submit to learn to hem a ruffle of his wife or his wife's maid; but if a mere wish could attain it, he would rather wish to be able to hem a ruffle.'

OLD AGE AND GOOD HUMOUR
'Why, Sir, a man grows better humoured as he grows older. He improves by experience. When young, he thinks himself of great consequence, and everything of importance. As he advances in life, he learns to think himself of no consequence, and little things of little importance; and so he becomes more patient and better pleased. All good-humour and complaisance are acquired. Naturally a child seizes directly what it sees, and thinks of pleasing itself only. By degrees, it is taught to please others, and to prefer others; and that this will ultimately produce the greatest happiness.'

EXPERIENCE

As I know more of mankind I expect less of them and am ready now to call a man a good man on easier terms.

COURAGE

'Courage is reckoned the greatest of all virtues; because, unless a man has that virtue, he has no security for preserving any other.'

SUICIDE AND COURAGE

I have often thought that after a man has taken the resolution to kill himself it is not courage in him to do anything, however desperate, because he has nothing to fear.

Goldsmith. 'I don't see that.'

Nay, but my dear Sir, why should you not see what everyone else sees?

Goldsmith. 'It is for fear of something that he has resolved to kill himself, and will not that timid disposition restrain him.

'It does not signify that the fear of something made him resolve. It is upon the state of his mind after the resolution is taken I argue. Supposing a man either from fear of pride or conscience or whatever motive has resolved to kill himself, when once the resolution is taken he has nothing to fear. He may then go and take the king of Prussia by the nose at the head of his army. He cannot fear the rack who is resolved to kill himself.

'When Eustace Budget* was walking down to the Thames determined to drown himself, he might if he pleased without any apprehension of danger have turned aside and first set fire to St. James's Palace.'

PEACE AND WAR

Mutual cowardice keeps us in peace. Were one half of mankind brave and one half cowards, the brave would always be

---

* Eustace Budget: Eustace Budgell (1686-1737), a journalist accused of forgery who committed suicide.

beating the cowards. Were all brave they would lead a very uneasy life, all would be continually fighting, but being all cowards we go on very well.

MEMORY
Pray, Sir, do you ever forget what money you are worth, and who gave you the last kick on the shins you had? Now if you would pay the same attention to what you read as you do to your temporal concerns and your bodily feelings, you would impress it as deeply on your memory.

UNFAIRLY TREATED
'There is a wicked inclination in most people to suppose an old man decayed in his intellect. If a young or middle-aged man, when leaving a company, does not recollect where he laid his hat, it is nothing; but if the same inattention is discovered in an old man, people will shrug up their shoulders and say, "his memory is going." '

OLD AGE
'There is nothing against which an old man should be so much upon his guard as putting himself to nurse.'

ITS LIMITATIONS
Sir, it is not true: what a man could once do he would always do, unless indeed by vicious indolence and compliance with the nephews and nieces who crowd round an old fellow and help to tuck him in till he, contented with the exchange of fame for ease, even resolves to let them set the pillows at his back, and gives no further proof of his existence than just to suck the jelly which prolongs it.

SPORTS
'How wonderfully well I have contrived to be idle without them.'

BEFORE MOTORS

'If I had no duties, and no reference to futurity, I would spend my life in driving briskly in a post-chaise with a pretty woman; but she should be one who could understand me, and would add something to the conversation.'

POSTING*

'Life has not many things better than this.'

TO TWO LADIES WHO MUCH COMMENDED THE OMISSION OF ALL BAD WORDS FROM HIS DICTIONARY

'What, my dears, then you have been looking for them?'

---

* Posting: i.e. driving in a post-chaise.

Criticism Personal and Literary

MRS. THRALE
I know nobody who blasts by praise as you do, for whenever there is exaggerated praise everybody is set against a character.

BOSWELL AS A TRAVELLING COMPANION
'Whose acuteness would help my inquiry, and whose gaiety of conversation and civility of manners are sufficient to counteract the inconveniences of travel, in countries less hospitable than we have passed.'

BOSWELL AS A CLUB CANDIDATE
'Sir, you got into our club by doing what a man can do. Several of the members wished to keep you out. Burke told me he doubted if you were fit for it: but, now you are in, none of them are sorry. Burke says that you have so much good humour naturally, it is scarce a virtue.' – *Boswell*. 'They were afraid of you, Sir, as it was you who proposed me.' – *Johnson*. 'Sir, they knew that if they refused you they'd probably never have got in another. I'd have kept them all out.'

BOSWELL'S FAME
No, there are but two ways of preserving fame, one by sugar, the other by salt. Now, as the sweet way, Bozzy, you are but little likely to attain, I would have you plunge in vinegar and get fairly pickled at once.

TOPHAM BEAUCLERK

Boswell. 'Beauclerk has a keenness of mind which is very uncommon.' *Johnson.* 'Yes, Sir; and everything comes from him so easily. It appears to me that I labour when I say a good thing.' *Boswell.* 'You are loud, Sir; but it is not an effort of mind.'

HIS CHARACTER

Thy body is all vice, thy mind all virtue! Nay, Sir, Alexander the Great marching in triumph into Babylon would not have desired to have more said of him.

SIR JOSHUA REYNOLDS

There goes a man unspoilt by success.

INVULNERABLE

Sir Joshua Reynolds, Sir, is the most invulnerable man I know. The man with whom if you should quarrel you would find the most difficulty how to abuse.

DR. HURD, BISHOP OF WORCESTER

Hurd, Sir, is one of a set of men who account for everything systematically. For instance, it has been a fashion to wear scarlet breeches, these men would tell that according to causes and effects no other wear could at that time have been chosen.

JOHN WESLEY, A GHOST, AND CHARLES

He can talk well on any subject.

Boswell. 'Pray, Sir, what has he made of his story of the ghost.'

Johnson. 'Why, Sir, he believes it, but not on sufficient authority. He did not take time enough to examine the girl. It was at Newcastle when the ghost was said to have appeared to a young woman several times, mentioning something about the right to the old house, advising application to an attorney, which was done, and at the same time saying the attorney would do nothing – which proved to be the fact. This, says John, is a proof that the ghost knows our thoughts. Now it is not necessary to know our thoughts to tell that an attorney will sometimes do nothing. Charles Wesley, who is a more stationary man, does not believe the story.'

SIR JOHN HAWKINS

As to Sir John, why I really believe him to be an honest man at the bottom, but to be sure he is penurious and he is mean, and it must be owned he has a degree of brutality, and a tendency to savageness that cannot easily be defended.

Sir John and I once belonged to the same club, but as he ate no supper after the first night of his admission he desired to be excused paying his share.

Sir John was a most unclubable man.

TOM DAVIES, WHO INTRODUCED BOSWELL TO DR. JOHNSON – AND AFTER FAILING AS A BOOKSELLER ADVENTURED AS AN AUTHOR

'An author generated by the corruption of a bookseller.'

DAVID GARRICK

No wonder, Sir, that he is vain – a man who is perpetually flattered in every mode than can be conceived – so many bellows have to trim the fire that one wonders by this time he is not become a cinder.

TO GARRICK'S MOTHER

Madam, David will either be hanged or become a great man.

HIS FAME

Oh, Sir, he deserves everything he has acquired for having seized the very soul of Shakespeare, for having embodied it in himself and for having expended its glory over the world.

WONDERFUL

'Sir, it is wonderful how little Garrick assumes. No, Sir!

Garrick *fortunam reverenter habet.* Consider, Sir: celebrated men such as you have mentioned have had their applause at a distance: but Garrick had it dashed in his face, sounded in his ears, and went home every night with the plaudits of a thousand in his cranium. Then, Sir, Garrick did not find but made his way to the tables, the levees, and almost the bed-chambers of the great. Then, Sir, Garrick had under him a numerous body of people who from fear of his power and hopes of his favour and admiration of his talents were constantly submissive to him, and here is a man who has advanced the dignity of his profession – Garrick has made a player a highest character.'

Scott. 'And he is a very sprightly writer too.'

Johnson. 'Yes, Sir, and all this is supported by great wealth of his own acquisition. If all this had happened to me I should have had a couple of fellows with long poles walking before me to knock down everyone that stood in the way.'

'Consider, if all this had happened to Cibber or Quin they'd have jumped over the moon – Yes, Garrick speaks to us.'

Boswell. 'And Garrick is a very good man, a charitable man.'

Johnson. 'Sir – a liberal man. He has given away more money than any man in England – there may be a little vanity mixed, but he has shown that money is not his first object.'

Boswell. 'Yet Foote used to say of him that he walked out with the intention of doing a generous action, but turning the corner of a street he met the ghost of a halfpenny which frightened him.'

Johnson. 'Why, Sir, that is very true too, for I never knew a man of whom it could be said with less certainty to-day what he will do to-morrow than Garrick. It depends so much on his humour at the time.'

Scott. 'I am glad to hear of his liberality, he has been represented as very saving.'

Johnson. 'With his domestic saving we have nothing to do. I remember drinking tea with him long ago when Peg

119

Woffington made it, and he grumbled at her for making it too strong.

'He had then begun to feel money in his purse and did not know when he should have enough of it.'

HIS CONVERSATION

Garrick's conversation is gay and grotesque. It is a dish of all sorts but all good things. There is no solid meat in it, there is a want of sentiment in it. Not but that he has sentiment sometimes and sentiment, too, very powerful and very pleasing, but it has not its full proportion in his conversation.

HIS ACTING

Garrick, madam, was no declaimer. There was not one of his own scene-shifters who could not have spoken 'To be or not to be' better than he did. Yet he was the only actor I ever saw whom I could call a master both in tragedy and comedy, though I liked him best in comedy. A fine conception of character and natural expression of it were his distinguished excellencies.

After all, madam, I thought him less to be envied on the stage than at the head of a table.

GARRICK AND THE KING

Sir, he has no right in a royal apartment to expect the hallooing and clamour of the one-shilling gallery. The King, I doubt not, gave him as much applause as was rationally his due; and indeed great and uncommon as is the merit of Mr. Garrick, no man will be bold enough to assert that he has not had his just proportion both of fame and profit. He has long reigned the unequalled favourite of the public, and therefore nobody, we may venture to say, will mourn his hard lot if the King and the Royal Family are not transported into rapture on hearing him read Lethe; but yet Mr. Garrick will complain to his friends and his friends will lament the King's want of feeling and taste, but then – Mr. Garrick will kindly excuse the King. He will say that

His Majesty might perhaps be thinking of something else! That the affairs of America might possibly occur to him, and some other subject of state more important perhaps than Lethe, but though he will candidly say this himself, he will not easily forgive his friends if they do not contradict him.

HIS THRIFT

Yes, Sir, I know that Garrick has given away more money than any man in England I am acquainted with, and that not from ostentatious views. Garrick was very poor when he began life, so when he came to have money he was probably very unskilful in giving away and saved where he should not; but Garrick began to be liberal as soon as he could, and I am of opinion this reputation of avarice which he has had has been very lucky for him and prevented his having many enemies. You despise a man for avarice, you do not hate him. Garrick might have been much better attacked for living with more splendour than is suitable to a player. If they had had the wit to have assaulted him in that quarter they might have galled him more, but they have kept clamouring about his avarice which has rescued him from much obloquy and envy.

HIS APPEARANCE

David looks much older than he is, for his face has had double the business of any other man's. It is never at rest, and when he speaks one minute he has quite a different countenance to what he assumes the next, and such an eternal restless fatiguing play of the muscles must certainly wear out a man s face before its real time.

SAMUEL FOOTE

The first time I was in company with Foote was at Fitzherbert's. Having no good opinion of the fellow I was resolved not to be pleased, and it is very difficult to please a man against his will. I went on eating my dinner pretty sullenly, affecting not to mind him. But the dog was so very comical that I was obliged to lay down my knife and fork, throw myself back upon my chair and fairly laugh it out. No, Sir, he was irresistible. He upon one occasion experienced in an extraordinary degree the efficacy of his powers of entertaining. Among the many and various modes which he tried of getting money he became a partner with a small-beer brewer, and he was to have a share of the profits for procuring customers amongst his numerous acquaintances. Fitzherbert was one who took his small beer, but it was so bad the servants resolved not to drink it. They were at some loss how to notify their resolution, being afraid of offending their master who they knew liked Foote much as a companion. At last they fixed upon a little black boy who was rather a favourite to be their deputy. Having invested him with the whole authority of the kitchen, he was to inform Mr. Fitzherbert in all their names upon a certain day that they would drink Foote's small beer no longer. On that day Foote happened to be dining at Fitzherbert's and this boy served at table. He was so delighted with Foote's stories and merriment and grimaces that when he went downstairs he told them: This is the finest man I have ever seen. I will not deliver your message; I will drink his small beer.

AN OAK STICK
What is the common price of an oak-stick.
Mr. Davies. 'Sixpence.'
Johnson. 'Why then, Sir, give me leave to send your servant to purchase me a shilling one. I'll have a double quantity, for I am told Foote means to talk me off as he calls it, and I am determined the fellow shall not do it with impunity.'

FOOTE IN IRELAND
Sir! I am glad to hear he was kicked in Dublin. He is rising in the world. When he was in England no one thought it worth while to kick him.

SHERIDAN'S FATHER

Why, Sir, Sherry is dull, naturally dull but it must have taken him a great deal of pains to become what we now see him. Such an excess of stupidity is not in nature.

THE ACTOR HENDERSON

Sir! I never did the man an injury, yet he would read his tragedy to me.

OLIVER GOLDSMITH

'The misfortune of Goldsmith in conversation is this: he goes on without knowing how he is to get off. His genius is great, but his knowledge is small. As they say of a generous man, it is a pity he is not rich, we may say of Goldsmith it is a pity he is not knowing. He would not keep his knowledge to himself.'

HIS MISTAKE

'Goldsmith should not be for ever attempting to shine in conversation: he has not temper for it, he is so much mortified when he fails. Sir, a game of jokes is composed partly of skill, partly of chance; a man may be beat at times by one who has not the tenth part of his wit. Now Goldsmith's putting himself against another, is like a man laying a hundred to one who cannot spare the hundred. It is not worth a man's while. A man should not lay a hundred to one, unless he can easily spare it, though he has a hundred chances for him: he can get but a guinea, and he may lose a hundred. Goldsmith is in this state. When he contends, if he gets the better, it is a very little addition to a man of his literary reputation: if he does not get the better, he is miserably vexed.'

THE RESULT

No man was more foolish when he had not a pen in his hand or more wise when he had.

ARGUMENT
'What Goldsmith comically says of himself is very true, – he always gets the better when he argues alone; meaning, that he is master of a subject in his study, and can write well upon it; but when he comes into company, grows confused, and unable to talk.'

HIS COMEDIES
'He who has written the two best comedies of his age, is surely a considerable man.'

'THE TRAVELLER'
'There has not been so fine a poem since Pope's time.'

HIS NATURAL HISTORY
'Goldsmith, Sir, will give us a very fine book upon the subject; but if he can distinguish a cow from a horse, that, I believe, may be the extent of his knowledge of natural history.'

AFTER HIS DEATH
If nobody was suffered to abuse poor Goldy but those who could write as well, he would have few censors.

LAURENCE STERNE
'Nay, Sir, any man who has a name, or who has the power of pleasing, will be very generally invited in London. The man, Sterne, I have been told, has had engagements for three months.'
Goldsmith. 'And a very dull fellow.'
Johnson. 'Why, no, Sir.'

HENRY FIELDING
Fielding being mentioned, Johnson exclaimed, 'He was a blockhead'; and upon my expressing my astonishment at so strange an assertion, he said, 'What I mean by his being a blockhead is, that he was a barren rascal.'
Boswell. 'Will you not allow, Sir, that he draws very natural pictures of human life?'

Johnson. 'Why, Sir, it is of very low life. Richardson used to say that had he not known who Fielding was, he should have believed he was an ostler. Sir, there is more knowledge of the heart in one letter of Richardson's than in all *Tom Jones*. I, indeed, never read *Joseph Andrews*.'

Erskine. 'Surely, Sir, Richardson is very tedious.'

Johnson. 'Why, Sir, if you were to read Richardson for the story, your impatience would be so much fretted that you would hang yourself. But you must read him for the sentiment, and consider the story as only giving occasion to the sentiment.'

AMELIA

Fielding's Amelia was the most pleasing heroine of all the romances, but that vile broken nose, never cured, ruined the sale of perhaps the only book which being printed off betimes one morning a new edition was called for before night.

FIELDING AND RICHARDSON

Sir, there is all the difference in the world between characters of nature and characters of manners, and there is the difference between the characters of Fielding and those of Richardson. Characters of manners are very entertaining, but they are to be understood by a more superficial observer than characters of nature, where a man must dive into the recesses of the human heart.

DISTINGUISHED

There is as great a difference between them as between a man who knew how a watch was made and a man who could tell the hour by looking on the dial-plate.

SAMUEL RICHARDSON

'An author who has enlarged the knowledge of human nature and taught the passions to move at the command of virtue.'

A FEMINIST

'His perpetual study was to ward off petty inconveniences and procure petty pleasures; that his love of continual superiority was such, that he took care to be always surrounded by women, who listened to him implicitly, and did not venture to controvert his opinions; and that his desire of distinction was so great, that he used to give large vails to the Speaker Onslow's servants, that they might treat him with respect.'

HIS FLATTERERS

That fellow died merely for want of change among his flatterers, he perished for want of more, like a man obliged to breathe the same air till exhausted.

HIS APPRECIATION

You think I love flattery – so I do, but a little too much always disgusts me. That fellow Richardson, on the contrary, could not be contented to sail quietly down the stream of reputation without longing to taste the froth from every stroke of the oar.

CORNEILLE

Corneille is to Shakespeare as a clipped hedge is to a forest.

STEELE'S ESSAYS

They are too thin for an Englishman's taste. Mere superficial observations on life and manners without erudition enough to make them keep, like the light French wines which turn sour for standing a while for want of body.

MISS BURNEY

Richardson would have been really afraid of her. There is merit in *Evelina* he could not have borne. No, it would not have done unless indeed she would have flattered him prodigiously. Harry Fielding, too, would have been afraid of her. There is nothing so delicately finished in all Harry Fielding's works as in *Evelina*.

'EVELINA'

Evelina seems a work that should result from long experience and deep and intimate knowledge of the world. Yet it has been written without either. Miss Burney is a real wonder; what she is she is intuitively. Dr. Burney told me she had had the fewest advantages of any of his daughters from some peculiar circumstances, and yet such has been her timidity that he himself had not any suspicion of her powers.

BET FLINT, OF WHOM MRS. WILLIAMS DID NOT APPROVE

Bet wrote her own life in verse, which she brought to me, wishing that I would furnish her with a preface to it. I used to say of her that she was generally slut and drunkard, occasionally whore and thief. She had however genteel lodgings, a spinet on which she played and a boy that walked before her chair. Poor Bet was taken upon a charge of stealing a counterpane and tried at the Old Bailey. The Chief Justice, who loved a wench, summed up favourably and she was acquitted. After which Bet said with a gay and satisfied air, 'Now that the counterpane is my own, I shall make a petticoat of it.'

CONGREVE

The description of the temple in the *Mourning Bride* is the finest poetical passage I have ever read. I recollect none in Shakespeare equal to it. Sir, this is not comparing Congreve on the whole with Shakespeare as on the whole, but only maintaining that Congreve has one finer passage than any that can be found in Shakespeare. Sir, a man may have no more than ten guineas in the world but he may have these ten guineas in one piece, and so have a finer piece than a man who has ten thousand pounds.

DRYDEN

When I was a young fellow I wanted to write the life of Dryden, and in order to get materials I applied to the only two persons then alive who had seen him. They were old Swenney and old Cibber.

Swenney's information was no more than this, that at Wills' coffee house Dryden had a particular chair for himself which was set by the fire in winter and was then called his winter chair, and that it was carried out for him to the balcony in summer and was then called his summer chair.

Cibber could tell no more but that he remembered him as a decent old man, arbiter of critical disputes at Wills'.

POPE AND DRYDEN ON THE FOLLOWING REMARK BY VOLTAIRE

'Pope drives a handsome chariot with a couple of neat trim nags. Dryden a coach and six stately horses.'

Johnson. 'Why, Sir, the truth is that they both drive coaches and six, but Dryden's horses are either galloping or stumbling. Pope's go at a steady, even trot.'

POPE

Sir, a thousand years may elapse before there shall appear another man with a power of versification equal to that of Pope.

MILTON'S SONNETS

Milton was a genius that could cut a colossus from a rock but could not carve heads upon cherry stones.

THE THREE BOOKS

How few books are there of which one ever can possibly arrive at the last page. Was there ever yet anything written by mere man that was wished longer by its readers excepting *Don Quixote, Robinson Crusoe* and the *Pilgrim's Progress*?

BURTON

Burton's *Anatomy of Melancholy* he said, was the only book

that ever took him out of bed two hours sooner than he wished
to rise.

ADDISON
Give nights and days to the study of Addison if you mean
either to be a good writer or what is more worth an honest man.

SWIFT
'Swift is clear, but he is shallow. In coarse humour he is
inferior to Arbuthnot; in delicate humour, he is inferior to
Addison: So he is inferior to his contemporaries; without putting
him against the whole world. I doubt if the *Tale of a Tub* was
his; it has so much more thinking, more knowledge, more power,
more colour, than any of the works which are indisputably his.
If it was his, I shall only say, he was *impar sibi*.'

GRAY
'Sir, I do not think Gray a first-rate poet. He has not a bold
imagination, nor much command of words. The obscurity in
which he has involved himself will not persuade us that he is
sublime. His *Elergy in a Church-yard* has a happy selection of
images, but I don't like what are called his great things.'

HIS DULNESS
'Sir, he was dull in company, dull in his closet, dull every-
where. He was dull in a new way, and that made many people
think him GREAT. He was a mechanical poet.'

MR. CAPELL, RIVAL EDITOR OF SHAKESPEARE
His abilities are just sufficient, Sir, to enable him to select
the black hairs from the white ones for the use of periwig makers.

THE RESPECTIVE MERITS OF DERRICK AND SMART AS POETS
'Sir, there is no settling the point of precedency between a
louse and a flea.'

KIT SMART

'It seems as if his mind had ceased to struggle with the disorder, for he grows fat upon it.'

Dr. Burney. 'Perhaps that may be from want of exercise.'

Johnson. 'No, Sir, he has partly as much exercise as he need to have, for he digs in the garden. Indeed, before his confinement he used for exercise to walk to the alehouse, but he was carried back again. I did not think he ought to be shut up. His infirmities were not noxious to society. He insisted on people praying with him, and I'd as lief pray with Kit Smart as anyone else. Another charge was he did not love clean linen and I have no passion for it.'

BURKE

'Yes; Burke is an extraordinary man. His stream of mind is perpetual.'

HIS DISTINCTION

Burke, Sir, is such a man, that if you met him for the first time in a street where you were stopped by a drove of oxen, and you and he stepped aside to take shelter but for five minutes, he'd talk to you in such a manner, that, when you parted, you would say, This is an extraordinary man. Now, you may be long enough with me without finding anything extraordinary.

HIS EFFECT

'That fellow calls forth all my powers. Were I to see Burke now it would kill me.'

BURKE AS A HUMORIST

'No, Sir; he never succeeds there. 'Tis low: 'tis conceit. I used to say Burke never once made a good joke. What I most envy Burke for, is his being constantly the same. He is never what we call hum-drum; never unwilling to begin to talk, nor in a haste to leave off.'

Boswell. 'Yet he can listen.'

Johnson. 'No; I cannot say he is good at that. So desirous is he to talk that, if one is speaking at this end of the table, he'll speak to somebody at the other end.'

COLLEY CIBBER

'Colley Cibber once consulted me as to one of his birthday Odes, a long time before it was wanted. I objected very freely to several passages. Cibber lost patience, and would not read his Ode to an end. When we had done with criticism, we walked over to Richardson's, the author of *Clarissa*, and I wondered to find Richardson displeased that I "did not treat Cibber with more *respect*." Now, Sir, to talk of *respect for a player*!'

SIR ROBERT WALPOLE

He was the best minister this country ever had. If we would have let him, he would have kept the country in perpetual peace.

CHARLES JAMES FOX

'Fox never talks in private company; not from any determination not to talk, but because he has not the first notion. A man who is used to the applause of the House of Commons has no wish for that of a private company. A man accustomed to throw for a thousand pounds, if set down to throw for sixpence would not be at the pains to count his dice. Burke's talk is the ebullition of his mind; he does not talk from a desire of distinction, but because his mind is full.'

AUT CÆESAR AUT NULLUS

Fox is a liberal man; he would always be *aut Cæsar aut nullus*. Whenever I have seen him he has been *nullus*.

PITT

I asked him if it was true as reported that he had said lately: 'I am for the King against Fox, but I am for Fox against Pitt.' *Johnson.* 'Yes, Sir, the King is my master, but I do not know Pitt and Fox as my friends. Fox is a most extraordinary man.

Here is a man who has divided the kingdom with Cæsar, so that it was a doubt whether the nation should be ruled by the sceptre of George III, or the tongue of Fox.'

JOHN WILKES

'Did we not hear so much said of Jack Wilkes, we should think more highly of his conversation. Jack has a great variety of talk, Jack is a scholar, and Jack has the manners of a gentleman. But after hearing his name sounded from pole to pole, as the phoenix of convivial felicity, we are disappointed in his company. He has always been *at me*: but I would do Jack a kindness, rather than not. The contest is now over.'

LORD NORTH

I am glad the ministry is removed. Such a bunch of imbecility never disgraced the country.

THE DUKE OF DEVONSHIRE

'He was not a man of superior abilities, but he was a man strictly faithful to his word. If, for instance, he had promised you an acorn, and none had grown that year in his woods, he would not have contented himself with that excuse: he would have sent to Denmark for it. So unconditional was he in keeping his word; so high as to the point of honour.'

LORD THURLOW

'Sir, it is when you come close to a man in conversation, that you discover what his real abilities are: to make a speech in a public assembly is a knack. Now I honour Thurlow, Sir; Thurlow is a fine fellow; he fairly put his mind to yours.'

THE ONLY ONE

'I would prepare myself for no man in England but Lord Thurlow. When I am to meet with him, I should wish to know a day before.'

THE POSTHUMOUS 'PHILOSOPHY' OF LORD BOLINGBROKE

'Sir, he was a scoundrel and a coward. A scoundrel for charging a blunderbus against religion and morality. A coward because he had no resolution to fire it off himself, but left half-a-crown to a beggarly Scotchman to draw the trigger after his death.'

GEORGE III

Sir, they may talk of the King as they will; he is the finest gentleman I ever saw.

LORD CHESTERFIELD

'This man (said he) I thought had been a Lord among wits; but, I find, he is only a wit among Lords.'

LORD CHESTERFIELD'S LETTERS TO HIS SON

'They teach the morals of a whore, and the manners of a dancing master.'

ON HIS TWO ESSAYS IN PRAISE OF JOHNSON JUST BEFORE THE PUBLICATION OF THE DICTIONARY

I have sailed a long and painful voyage round the world of the English language, and does he now send two cockboats to tow me into harbour?

ROUSSEAU

'Sir, if you are talking jestingly of this, I don't talk with you. If you mean to be serious, I think him one of the worst of men; a rascal, who ought to be hunted out of society, as he has been. Three or four nations have expelled him; and it is a shame that he is protected in this country.'

HIS HONESTY

'Sir, that will not do. We cannot prove any man's intention to be bad. You may shoot a man through the head, and say you intended to miss him; but the judge will order you to be hanged. An alleged want of intention, when evil is committed, will not be allowed in a court of justice. Rousseau, Sir, is a very bad man. I would sooner sign a sentence for his transportation, than that of any felon who has gone from the Old Bailey these many years. Yes, I should like to have him work in the plantations.'

AS COMPARED WITH VOLTAIRE
'Why, Sir, it is difficult to settle the proportion of iniquity between them.'

ON A CERTAIN MR. FLEXMAN
Sir, let me hear no more of him. That is the fellow who made the index to my *Ramblers*, and set down the name of Milton thus: Milton, Mr. John.

FREDERICK THE GREAT
As to his being an author, I have not looked at his poetry, but his prose is poor stuff. He writes just as you would suppose Voltaire's foot-boy to do who has been his amanuensis. He has such parts as the valet might have, and about as much of the colouring of the style as might be got by transcribing his works.

MANKIND
From my experience I have found them worse in commercial dealings, more disposed to cheat than I had any notice of, but more disposed to do one another good than I had conceived – and really it is wonderful, considering how much attention is necessary for men to take care of themselves and ward off immediate evils which press upon them, it is wonderful how much they do for others. As it is said of the greatest liar that he tells more truth than falsehood, so it may be said of the worst man that he does more good than evil.

Precept and Practice, and Religion

PRACTISING WHAT YOU PREACH
'Sir, are you so grossly ignorant of human nature as not to know that a man may be very sincere in good principles without having good practice?'

PRACTICE AND PRECEPT
'I cannot help that, Madam. That does not make his book the worse. People are influenced more by what a man says, if his practice is suitable to it – because they are blockheads. The more intellectual people are, the readier they will attend to what a man tells them. If it is just, they will follow it, be his practice what it will. No man practises so well as he writes. I have, all my life long, been lying till noon; yet I tell all young men, and tell them with great sincerity, that nobody who does not rise early will ever do any good. Only consider! You read a book: you are convinced by it; you do not know the author. Suppose you afterwards know him, and find that he does not practice what he teaches; are you to give up your former conviction? At this rate you would be kept in a state of equilibrium, when reading every book, till you knew how the author practised.'

PRACTICE
The happiest part of a man's life is what he passes lying awake in bed in the morning.

MERE PURPOSE
Life, to be worthy of a rational being, must be always in progression; we must always propose to do more or better than

in time past. The mind is enlarged and elevated by mere purposes, though they end as they began, by airy contemplation. We compare and judge, though we do not practise.

CATHOLICS

On the Roman Catholic religion he said, 'If you join the Papists externally, they will not interrogate you strictly as to your belief in their tenets. No reasoning Papist believes every article of their faith. There is one side on which a good man might be persuaded to embrace it. A good man of a timorous disposition, in great doubt of his acceptance with God, and pretty credulous, may be glad to be of a church where there are so many helps to get to Heaven. I would be a Papist if I could. I have fear enough; but an obstinate rationality prevents me. I shall never be a Papist, unless on the near approach of death, of which I have a very great terror. I wonder that women are not all Papists.'

VOW

'What? a vow – O, no, Sir, a vow is a horrible thing, it is a snare for sin. The man who cannot go to heaven without a vow – may go – ' Here standing erect, in the middle of his library, and rolling grand, his pause was truly a curious compound of the solemn and the ludicrous; he half-whistled in his usual way, when pleasant, and he paused, as if checked by religious awe. Methought he would have added – to Hell.

CONSCIENCE

Conscience is nothing more than a conviction felt by ourselves of something to be done and something to be avoided, and in questions of simple, unperplexed morality conscience is very often a guide that may be trusted; but before conscience can determine, the state of the question is supposed to be completely known. In questions of law or of fact conscience is very often confounded with opinion. No man's conscience can tell him the rights of another man. They must be known by rational investigation or historical enquiry.

PURGATORY

I proceeded: 'What do you think, Sir, of Purgatory, as believed by the Roman Catholics?'

Johnson. 'Why, Sir, it is a very harmless doctrine. They are of opinion that the generality of mankind are neither so obstinately wicked as to deserve everlasting punishment, nor so good as to merit being admitted into the society of blessed spirits; and therefore that God is graciously pleased to allow of a middle state, where they may be purified by certain degrees of suffering. You see, Sir, there is nothing unreasonable in this.'

Boswell. 'But then, Sir, their masses for the dead?'

Johnson. 'Why, Sir, if it be once established that there are souls in purgatory, it is as proper to pray for *them*, as for our brethren of mankind who are yet in this life.'

Boswell. 'The idolatry of the Mass?'

Johnson. 'Sir, there is no idolatry in the Mass. They believe God to be there, and they adore him.'

Boswell. 'The worship of saints?'

Johnson. 'Sir, they do not worship saints; they invoke them; they only ask their prayers.'

CONFESSION

Boswell. 'Confession?'

Johnson. 'Why, I don't know but that is a good thing. The Scripture says, "Confess your faults one to another," and the priests confess as well as the laity. Then it must be considered that their absolution is only upon repentance, and often upon penance also. You think your sins may be forgiven without penance upon repentance alone." '

PROTESTANTISM

'A man who is converted from Protestantism to Popery may be sincere: he parts with nothing: he is only superadding to what he already had. But a convert from Popery to Protestantism gives up so much of what he has held as sacred as anything that he retains; there is so much *laceration of mind* in such a conversion, that it can hardly be sincere and lasting.'

ROME
'You are going where the ostentatious pomp of church ceremonies attracts the imagination; but if they want to persuade you to change, you must remember, that by increasing your faith, you may be persuaded to become Turk.'

CONVENTS
'It is as unreasonable for a man to go into a Carthusian convent for fear of being immoral, as for a man to cut off his hands for fear he should steal. There is, indeed, great resolution in the immediate act of dismembering himself: but when that is once done, he has no longer any merit: for though it is out of his power to steal, yet he may all his life be a thief in his heart. So when a man has once become a Carthusian, he is obliged to continue so, whether he chooses it or not. Their silence, too, is absurd. We read in the Gospel of the apostles being sent to preach, but not to hold their tongues. All severity that does not tend to increase good, or prevent evil, is idle. I said to the Lady Abbess of a Convent, "Madam, you are here not for the love of virtue, but the fear of vice." She said, "She should remember this as long as she lived." '

ON ENTERING A RELIGIOUS RETREAT
'Yes, when he has done his duty to society. In general, as every man is obliged not only to "love God, but his neighbour as himself," he must bear his part in active life; yet there are exceptions. Those who are exceedingly scrupulous (which I do not approve, for I am no friend to scruples), and find their scrupulosity invincible, so that they are quite in the dark, and know not what they shall do – or those who cannot resist

temptations, and find they make themselves worse by being in the world, without making it better may retire. I never read of a hermit but in imagination I kiss his feet; never of a monastery, but I could fall on my knees and kiss the pavement. But I think putting young people there, who know nothing of life, nothing of retirement, is dangerous and wicked. It is a saying as old as Hesiod:

'Let active enterprise the young engage,
The riper man be famed for counsel sage;
Prayer is the proper duty of old age.

'That is a very noble line: not that young men should not pray, or old men not give counsel, but that every season of life has its proper duties. I have thought of retiring, and have talked of it to a friend; but I find my vocation is rather to active life.'

He said, 'If convents should be allowed at all, they should only be retreats for persons unable to serve the public, or who have served it. It is our first duty to serve society; and, after we have done that, we may attend wholly to the salvation of our own souls. A youthful passion for abstracted devotion should not be encouraged.'

GRACE BEFORE MEALS

'It is enough if we have stated seasons of prayer: no matter when. A man may as well pray when he mounts his horse, or a woman when she milks her cow (which Mr. Grant told us is done in the Highlands), as at meals; and custom is to be followed.'

FREE WILL

'Sir, we *know* our will is free, and *there's* an end on't.'

THE SUCCESS OF METHODISTS

Sir, it is owing to their expressing themselves in a plain and familiar manner which is the only way to do good to the common people, and which clergymen of genius and learning ought to do from a principle of duty when it is suited to their congregation, a practice for which they will be praised by men of sense. To insist against drunkenness as a crime because it debases reason, the noblest faculty of man, would be of no service to the common people, but to tell them they may die in a fit of drunkenness cannot fail to make a deep impression. Sir, when your Scotch clergy give up their homely manner, religion will soon decay in that country.

ON SALVATION BY FAITH ALONE
'Sir, there is no trusting to that crazy piety.'

RELIGION AND WOMEN
A principle of honour or fear of the world will many times keep a man in decent order, but when a woman loses her religion she in general loses the very tie that will restrain her actions.

SUNDAY
'It should be different from another day. People may walk, but not throw stones at birds. There may be relaxation, but there should be no levity.'

TO A GENTLEMAN WHO OBJECTED TO BIRD-CATCHING AT STREATHAM ON A SUNDAY
While half the Christian world is permitted to dance and sing and celebrate Sunday as a day of festivity, how comes your puritanical spirit so offended with frivolous and empty deviations from exactness?

CONSCIENCE AND ALGEBRA
A person had for these last five weeks often called at my door, but would not leave his name or other message but that he wished to speak with me. At last we met, and he told me he was oppressed by scruples of conscience. I blamed him gently for not applying as the rules of our church direct to his parish priest

or other discreet clergyman, when after some compliments on his part he told me that he was clerk to a very eminent trader at whose warehouse much business consists in packing goods to go abroad. That he was often tempted to take paper and pack-thread enough for his own use, and that he had indeed done so so often that he could recollect no time when he had bought anything for himself. But probably (said I) your master was wholly indifferent to such trivial emoluments. You had better ask for it at once and so take your trifles with consent. Oh, Sir, replies the visitor, my master bids me have as much as I please and was half angry when I talked to him about it. Then, pray Sir (said I), harry me no more about such airy nothings, and was giving on to be very angry, when I recollected the fellow might be mad perhaps, so I asked him when he left the counting-house of an evening. At 7 o'clock, Sir. And when do you go to bed, Sir? At twelve o'clock. Then (replied I) I have at least learnt this much by my new acquaintance, that five hours out of the twenty-four unemployed are enough for a man to go mad in, so I would advise you, Sir, to study Algebra if you are not an adept already in it. Your head would get less muddy and you will leave off tormenting your neighbours about paper and pack-thread while we all live together in a world bursting with sin and sorrow.

Death and His Own

THOUGHTS OF DEATH
'Sir, I had an uncle who died so; but such attention requires great leisure, and great firmness of mind. If one was to think constantly of death, the business of life would stand still. I am no friend to making religion appear too hard. Many good people have done harm by giving severe notions of it. In the same way, as to learning: I never frighten young people with difficulties; on the contrary, I tell them that they may very easily get as much as will do very well. I do not indeed tell them that they will be *Bentleys*.'

THE FUTURE
'You know I never thought confidence, with respect to futurity, any part of the character of a brave, a wise, or a good man. Bravery has no place where it can avail nothing; wisdom impresses strongly the consciousness of those faults, of which it is, perhaps, itself an aggravation; and goodness, always wishing to be better and imputing every deficiency to criminal negligence, and every fault to voluntary corruption, never dares to suppose the condition of forgiveness fulfilled, nor what is wanting in the crime supplied by penitence.

'This is the state of the best; but what must be the condition of him whose heart will not suffer him to rank himself among the best, or among the good? – Such must be his dread of the approaching trial, as will leave him little attention to the opinion of those whom he is leaving for ever; and serenity that is not felt it can be no virtue to feign.'

PREPARING FOR THE END

No, Sir, let it alone. It matters not how a man dies but how he lives. The act of dying is not of importance, it lasts so short a time. A man knows it must be so and submits. It will do him no good to whine.

DISTRACTION

The whole of life is but keeping away the thoughts of death.

NECESSARY

If one was to think constantly of death the business of life would stand still.

ITS TERROR

I have never had a moment in which death was not terrible to me. It has been observed that scarcely any man dies in public but with apparent resolution from that desire of praise which never quits us. (I said Dr. Dodd seemed to be willing to die and full of hopes of happiness.) Sir, Dr. Dodd would have given both his hands and both his legs to have lived. The better a man is the more afraid is he of death, having a clearer view of infinite purity.

FOR A RATIONAL MAN

No rational man can die without uneasy apprehension.

HIMSELF

I have made no approaches to a state which can look on it as not terrible.

VIOLENT DEATH

A violent death is never very painful; the only danger is lest it should be unprovided; but if a man can be supposed to make no provision for death in war, what can be the state which would have awakened him to the care of futurity? When would that man have prepared himself to die who went to seek death without preparation? What, then, can be the reason why we lament more him that dies of a wound than him that dies of a fever? A man that languishes with disease ends his life with more pain, but with less virtue; he leaves no example to his friends, nor bequeathes any honour to his descendants. The only reason why we lament a soldier's death is that we think he might have lived longer. Yet this cause of grief is common to many other kinds of death which are not so passionately bewailed. The truth is every death is violent which is the effect of accident, every death which is not gradually brought on by the miseries of age, or where life is extinguished for any other reason than that it is burnt out. He that dies before sixty of a cold or a consumption dies in reality by a violent death, yet his death is borne with patience only because the cause of his untimely end is silent and invisible.

THE WIDOWER

He that outlives a wife whom he has long loved sees himself disjoined from the only mind that has the same hopes, fears, and interest, from the only companion with whom he has shared much good and evil, and with whom he could see his mind at liberty to retrace the past or anticipate the future. The continuity of being is lacerated: the settled course of sentiment and action is stopt, and life stands suspended and motionless till it is driven by external causes into a new channel, but the time of suspense is dreadful. Our first recourse in this distressed solitude is perhaps for want of habitual piety to a gloomy acquiescence in necessity. Of two mortal beings, one must lose the other, but surely there is a higher and a better comfort to be drawn from the consideration of that Providence which watches over all and a belief that the living and the dead are equally in the hands of God, who will reunite those whom he has separated, or sees that it is best not to reunite.

THE DEATH OF HIS WIFE

You know poor Mr. Dodsley has lost his wife. I hope he

will not suffer so much as I yet suffer for the loss of mine.

Οιμοι τι δ'οιμοι; θνηια γαρ πεπονθα μεν

I have ever since seemed to myself broken off from mankind, a kind of solitary wanderer in the wild of life without any direction or fixed point of view. A gloomy gazer on a world to which I have little relation.

HUME'S DEATH
Why should it shock you, Sir? Hume owned he had never read the New Testament with attention. Here, then, was a man who had been at no pains to inquire into the truth of religion and had continually turned his mind the other way. It was not to be expected that the prospect of death would alter his way of thinking, unless God should send an angel to set him right. (I said I had reason to believe that the thought of annihilation gave Hume no pain.)

It was not so, Sir. He had a vanity in being thought easy. It is more probable he should assume an appearance of ease than so very improbable a thing should be as a man not afraid of going (as in spite of his delusive theory he cannot be sure but he may go into an unknown state), and not being uneasy at leaving all he knew, and you are to consider that upon his own principle of annihilation he had no motive to speak the truth.

HIS LAST ILLNESS
'I will be conquered; I will not capitulate.'

HIS NURSE AND HOW HE LIKED HIM
'Not at all, Sir. The fellow is an idiot, he is as awkward as a turnspit when first put into the wheel and as sleepy as a dormouse.'

HIS PILLOW
'That will do – all that a pillow can do.'

ON RECEIVING HIS LAST LETTER
'An odd thought strikes me: – we shall receive no letters in the grave.'

TO GOOD WISHES
No, Sir! You cannot conceive with what acceleration I advance towards death.

ON LEARNING HIS CRITICAL CONDITION
'Then I will take no more physic, not even my opiates; for I have prayed that I may render up my soul to God unclouded.'

HIS LAST WORDS
'God bless you, my dear!'

Index

Accounts, 99
Actors, 39
Addison, Joseph, 129
Advocacy, 32-4
Algebra, 140-1
Amelia, 125
Americans, 85
Anatomy of Melancholy, The
   128-9
Antiquaries, 35
Appetite, 67
Arithmetic, 12
Army, The, 37
Aston, Molly, 19-20
Attorneys, 35
Authors, 35-7

Babies, 11
Banking, 97
Barclay and Perkins, 40
Baretti, Giuseppe, 47
Bargains, 43, 101
Barnard, Dr., 58
Bathurst, Earl, 88
Beauclerk, Topham, 117
Beauty, 21-2
Beggars, 111
Being hanged, 102
Biography, 111
Blockheads, Athenian, 87

Bishops and Clergy, 39-40
Boarding-schools, 16
Bolingbroke, Lord, 133
Booksellers, 109
Bores, 102
Boswell, James, 116
Brandy, 65
Bulldogs, 107
Burke, Edmund, 88, 130
Burney, Fanny, 126-7
Burton, Robert, 128-9

Cant, 92
Capell, Edward, 129
Card playing, 107
Careless, Mrs., 19
Cathedral society, 62-3
Catholics, 137-8
Charing Cross, 78
Charlemont, Lord, 87
Charles V, 74
Chesterfield, Earl of, 133
Children, 14, 16, 17, 25-6, 73
Children and Education, 14, 16,
   17
China, Great Wall of, 87
Cibber, Colley, 128, 131
Circus Riders, 39
Civil suicide, 44
Claret, 64-5

Clean linen, 130
Climate, 74
Climbers, social, 49
College friends, 45
Commandment, Seventh, 26
Complaisance, 26-7
Condescension, 107
Confession, 137
Congreve, William, 127
Conscience, 140
Contradiction, 54, 58
Controversy, 89-90
Convents, 138
Conversation, 50, 62, 102
Cookery Books, 70
Corneille, Pierre, 126
Corn Laws, 96
Country Life, 78-9
Courage, 113-14
Criticism, 36-7

Davies, Tom, 47, 118
Death, 142ff.
Debts, 99-100
Delicacy, 105
Derrick, Samuel, 129
Description, literary, 103
Devonshire, Duke of, 132
Dictionary, The, 108-9, 115
Dining, 65-6
Dinner parties, 68
Disobedience, 104
Dodsley, Robert, 144-5
Don Quixote, 128
Dress allowance, 24
Drinking, 60-1
Dryden, John, 128

Early hours, 108
Eating, 65-8
Eating and drinking, 60ff.
Education, 12-15
Elections, 90
Emigration, 87
Epitaphs, 110
Equality, social, 93-4
Evelina, 127
Exaggeration, 55-6

Faith, 140
Falling in love, 20-1
Family ties, 41-2
Fear, 74, 143
Fielding, Henry, 124-5
Finery, 105
Flattery, 50, 52
Flexman, Roger, 134
Flint, Bet, 127
Flogging, 14
Florence, wine from, 65
Fops, 105
Foote, Samuel, 121-2
Fortune hunters, 28
Fox, Charles James, 131
France, 68-9
Frederick the Great, 134
Free speech, 92
Free Trade, 96
Free will, 139
Friendship, 45ff.
Future, the, 142

Gambling, 42-3
Garrick, David, 118-21
Generosity, 44
George III, 59, 109, 133

Index

Ghosts, 110, 117
Giant's-Causeway, 87
Goldsmith, Oliver, 123-4
Gordon, Sir Alexander, 110-11
Grace, 139
Graces, The, 112
Gray, Thomas, 129

Happiness, 71ff.
Hardness, 74
Hawkins, Sir John, 118
Headache, 64
Hell, 137
Henderson, Andrew, 123
Hereditary rank, 94
Heresies, 107
Highlands, 83
Historians, 36
Home Rule, 85
Hume, David, 145
Hurd, Dr., 117
Husbands and Wives, 27

Idleness, 30
Illness, Johnson's last, 145-6
Imagination, 29
Impressions, early, 16
Infants, reciting, 17
Invasion, 53-4
Inverary, 104
Ireland, 84-5
Irish, the, 84
Italy, 86

Johnson, Mrs., 18-20, 144-5
Judges, 34

Kindness, 43

Knowledge, 112
Law, 34
Learning, 15, 100
Lectures, 13
Leisure, 34, 43
Lemons, 66
Liars, 55-6, 64
Liberty, 91
London, 77ff.
London and love, 78
Love, 20-1, 35, 78
Luxury, 100-1

Macaulay, Mrs., 94
Macleod, Lady, 67
Madness, 111
Mankind, 87, 113, 134
Manners, 37-8, 58
Marriage, generally, 21, 22ff.
Marriage, Johnson's, 18
Marriage, late, 25
Marriage, second, 25
Marriage Service, 21
Marrying a fool, 24
Marrying a student, 24-5
Marrying beneath one, 24
Mediterranean, the, 86
Melancholy, 75
Memory, 15, 106, 114
Men of the world, 106
Methodists, 139-40
Milton, John, 128
Mirth, 52
Misfortune, the greatest, 30
Monboddo, Lord, 110
Money, 97-9
Money-making, 31, 43
Montague, Mrs., 102

149

Mourning Bride, The, 127
Music, 30-1
Mystery, 105

Narrowness, 99
National character, 54, 102
New Rich, 41
North, Lord, 132
'Not at home,' 110
Nurse, Johnson's, 145

Old age, 104-5, 114
Old age pensions, 98
Old men, children of, 25-6
Opiates, 146
Orchards, 67

Parliament, 92
Parties, political, 89
Party spirit, 89
Pastern, defined, 109
Patriotism, 40
Peace, 113-14
Pension, Johnson's, 109
Petitions, 90
Piety, 105
Pigs, 104
Pilgrim's Progress, The, 128
Pillow, Johnson's, 145
Pitt, William, 131-2
Pity, 73
Pleasures, 108
Politeness, 45, 58
Pope, Alexander, 128
Popery, 137-8
Port, 61, 65
Portrait, 107
Posting, 115

Practice, 135
Precept, 135
Presents, 24
Prize ring, 43
Profession, choice of, 31
Protestantism, 137-8
Public schools, 12-13
Pulteney, George, 88
Punishment, 13-14
Purgatory, 137

Quarrels, 25
Quotation, 51

Ranelagh, 71
Readers, 15
Reading, 12, 14-15
Refinement, in education, 13
Relations, 45
Retreats, religious, 138-9
Republicanism, 94
Reynolds, Sir Joshua, 117
Richardson, Samuel, 125-6, 131
Robinson Crusoe, 128
Rome, 138
Rousseau, 133-4

Sailors, 38
St. Kilda, 83
Saving, 98-9
Scenery, 87
Schoolmasters, 17
Scotchmen, 81-5
Scotland, 81-3
Sculptors, 39
'Sensible man', defined, 102
Sheridan, Thomas, 123
Skipping, 108

Ships, 38
Smart, Christopher, 129-30
Smith, Adam, 97
Socialism, 93
Society, success in, 48-9
Solitude, 75
Sorrow, 72
Specialists, 112
Sport, 114
Stage doors, 103
Steele, Sir Richard, 126
Sterne, Laurence, 124
Study, 103
Suicide, 107, 113
Sunday, 140
Swift, Jonathan, 129

Tariff Reform, 96
Taverns, 40, 69
Tea, 67
Temperance, 60-1
Thrale, Mr., 53
Thrale, Mrs., 18, 116
Thurlow, Lord, 132
Timidity, in boys, 13
Trade, rivalry in, 41
Travel, 86f.
Truth, 12, 56-7, 110

Unions, 89

Valetudinarian, comments on, 49
Verbosity, 52-3, 107
Versatility, 44
Violin-playing, 31
Voltaire, 134
Vows, 136

Waiting for dinner, on, 57
Walpole, Sir Robert, 131
War, 38
Wealth, 97-8
Wesley, Charles, 117-8
Wesley, John, 117-8
Whigs, 88
Whigs and some politicks, 88ff.
Whisky, 82
Wickedness, 104-5
Widower, 144
Wilkes, John, 132
Windham, William, 32
Wine, 60-1, 64
Wits, 53
Women, 21ff., 35-6, 62, 106
Work, and the professions, 30ff.
World, the, 111
Writing, 35
    Letters, 48-9

Youth, 45-6